DISCOVERY OF THE YOSEMITE

*reprinted from "Discovery of the Yosemite and
The Indian War of 1851 which led to that event"
first published in 1880
by Lafayette Bunnell*

LAFAYETTE BUNNELL

Copyright © 1980 OUTBOOKS, 217 Kimball Ave., Golden, Colorado 80401

ISBN 0-89646-021-5

"The High Falls" (Yosemite Falls) *by Thomas Ayres, 1855*

*Thomas Ayres visited Yosemite Valley in 1855 and 1856 and sketched the first views of it. All 9 of these are reproduced throughout this book, through the courtesy of the Yosemite Museum and the National Park Service. They get the credit for all other photographs, too. Period engravings come from **Picturesque California** (1888) edited by John Muir, **America Illustrated** (1883), **Scribner's** (1872, 1878), and **Century** (1890). The Bancroft Library of the University of California assisted with others.*

CONTENTS

Major James D. Savage
leader of Mariposa Battalion
during discovery of Yosemite Valley

EDITOR'S PREFACE: an historical perspective

Bunnell's "Discovery of the Yosemite" is valuable from many standpoints — the discovery and naming of the most remarkable valley on Earth, the conflicts between Indians and whites that inevitably arose throughout America, the methods of warfare used in the 1850 California frontier, and the lifestyles of the natives and the miners.

The current text is printed from the fourth edition of 1911 — same as the third, which corrected errors that were in the second edition and the first (1880). Here only those parts of the original work that relate directly to the discovery of Yosemite are reproduced, along with near-contemporary drawings and photographs, in the belief that such a format will best serve the interests of park visitors.

Today the geographic term Mariposa excites little interest, calling to mind at most an unimposing foothill town along one of the roads leading to Yosemite National Park and, perhaps, a giant sequoia grove. In 1851, however, Mariposa was a brand new and booming gold center, where Kit Carson had just discovered the Mother Lode and John and Bessie Fremont were developing their huge estate nearby in competition with gold-seeking '49er squatters. California, just wrested from Mexico, had been a State only 4 months when the Mariposa Battalion was mustered into service. The time was one of intense change with fierce competition among mining, trading, and agricultural interests — as well as between the original claimants of the land and their latest challengers.

This history precedes that of the classic American Indian Wars period. Custer fought last in 1876, for instance, and the Wounded Knee battle was as late as 1890 — and still going on! The reason is that California was destined to be developed prior to other parts of the West — it could be reached by sea around Cape Horn or with a shortcut across narrow Panama; with both water and a long growing season its agricultural potential was immensely greater; its climate was more favorable to habitation; transportation was possible on its inland bays and rivers; the lowland Indians were already tamed; and its gold deposits were discovered early and were easy to get to and to mine.

In 1851, the Civil War had not been fought to nationalize the principle of racial equality, and there was no railroad or telegraph west of the Mississippi River. The horse was the method of travel and communication everywhere and of transportation, too, in the uplands; and the gun plus vigilance the method of security.

Our chronicler, Dr. Lafayette Houghton Bunnell, was born in New York in 1824, making him about 27 years old when he enlisted in the Mariposa Battalion. After the Indian war he stayed in the Yosemite region several years engaged in water surveys, doctoring, and trading, but by about 1856 was settled permanently in the little town of Homer on the Minnesota-Wisconsin stateline. There he continued his medical and military pursuits, being listed when he died as "Late Surgeon, 36th Regiment, Wisconsin Volunteers", and there he wrote his Yosemite memoirs.

There was a current chronicler of the Battalion's activities at Yosemite — Adjutant Lewis, but Bunnell dismisses his report, noting in the September 1890 *Century Magazine* "At the date of the discovery of the Yosemite our adjutant was not with us. As we were broken up into scouting squads, an adjutant would have been no more useful in hunting Indians than would have been a drum major," Further, Bunnell discredits the adjutant's principal source of information — no less than their leader Major Savage — who was "talented, but unlettered and was dependent on his adjutant for all written communications and these were frequently made long after the events . . . The character of Major Savage's reports may be judged by his official estimate of the number of Indians engaged in hostilities (23,000)."

Thus, although some of the trip's freshness must already have faded from Bunnell's mind by the time he began writing, and some of his perspectives must have changed, still his account is the only first-hand record left by any of the group of soldiers who first entered the valley.

In doing his research on names, dates, etc., Bunnell found "nothing in the archives of California that could aid him." To one of his inquiries, the Adjutant-General of California replied "The records of this office both written and printed, are so incomplete that I am not aware, from consulting them, that the organization to which you allude had any existence." Later researches have been more successful at finding letters, diaries, etc., and so some of Bunnell's dates have been revised with footnotes in the present edition.

In fact, there had even been prior discoveries of Yosemite Valley. The Indians would argue correctly that theirs was the first, and they also participated as guides for many of the early trips past and into the gorge. The first of these was that of Joseph Walker, en route through the region as part of an extensive search for beaver in the West.

Walker's discovery took place in October of 1833. The fact of it was unknown to Yosemite Valley's early historians, however, as the record was published obscurely. Walker himself may not have looked down into the valley, although some of his party — perhaps scouts — clearly did so, and probably also saw Hetch Hetchy Valley. His clerk Zenas Leonard told it:

> We travelled a few miles every day, still on top of the mountain, and our course continually obstructed with snow hills and rocks. Here we began to encounter in our path many small streams which would shoot out from under these high snow-banks, and after running a short distance in deep chasms which they have through the ages cut in the rocks, precipitate themselves from one lofty precipice to another, until they are exhausted in rain below. Some of these precipices appeared to us to be more than a mile high. Some of the men thought that if we could succeed in descending one of these precipices to the bottom, we might thus work our way into the valley below — but on making several attempts we found it utterly impossible for a man to descend, to say nothing of our horses. We were then obliged to keep along the top of the dividing ridge between two of these chasms which seemed to lead pretty near in the direction we were going — which was west, — in passing over the mountain, supposing it to run north and south.

Another "discovery" of Yosemite Valley was made in 1849 by W.P. Abrams and U.N. Reamer, while returning from a grizzly bear hunt. In his diary, Abrams described a valley 3,000 feet deep with a mountain that looked "as though it had been sliced with a knife."

Bunnell himself in 1849 had seen El Capitan from afar:

> In the distance an immense cliff loomed . . . I looked upon this awe-inspiring column with wonder and admiration . . . I turned from it with reluctance to resume the search for coveted gold.

On entering the valley with the Battalion over a year later, Bunnel "saw at a glance that the reality of my sublime vision . . . forty miles away, was before me."

Doubtless there were others who saw the unusual place from near or far in these early years, but never mentioned it where posterity would hear. Neither Bunnell nor the Battalion did anything to popularize the valley, yet the knowledge of the area they gained and the improvements they made to it in safety of travel (by removing the Indians) did facilitate further trips and lead to publicity that established it early throughout the world as a remarkable locality. In fact, within just 13 years and while in the midst of civil war, a young nation became the first in the world to deliberately preserve part of its domain as a natural area for public use, and Yosemite Valley became a "National Park" (as Bunnell called it) . . . deemed entirely worthy of this great republic and of the great Golden State that has accepted its guardianship."

And so Bunnell persevered and produced his record for the world. For having done so and also for having recognized Yosemite's superlative qualities and expressed his opinion in defense of them, his fellow doctors later commemorated him with a plaque. If you search, you can still find it — on a large granite boulder beside the meadow and river where, beside their first campfire, the young doctor and his soldier companions discussed the valley and chose its name.

Today's world finds Bunnell's story still meaningful, and hopefully they will find in Bunnell a man charitable with respect to the scenery, his companions, and the Indians — albeit constrained by the philosophical limitations of his time.

William R. Jones
former Chief Park Naturalist
Yosemite National Park

JOSEPH R. WALKER

AUTHOR'S INTRODUCTION
by Lafayette Houghton Bunnell

The book here presented is the result of an attempt to correct existing errors relative to the Yosemite Valley. It was not deemed just that California should forget the deeds of men who had subdued her savages, and discovered her most sublime scenery. Having been a member of the "Mariposa Battalion," and with it when the Yosemite was discovered, having suggested its name, and named many of the principal objects of interest in and near the valley, it seemed a duty that the writer owed his comrades and himself, to give the full history of these events. Many of the facts incident thereto have already been given to the public by the author at various times since 1851, but these have been so mutilated or blended with fiction, that a renewed and full statement of facts concerning that remarkable locality seems desirable.

His especial efforts have been directed to the placing on record events connected with the *discovery* of the Yosemite, for description of its scenery he feels to be impossible.

Now a few facts in regard to the Discovery of the Yosemite Valley by Capt. Joseph Reddeford Walker, for whom Walker's River, Lake and Pass were named. It is not a new claim, as supposed and was set up in the *San Jose Pioneer* soon after Capt. Walker's death, and answered by me in the same paper in 1880.

I cheerfully concede the fact set forth in the *Pioneer* article that, "*His were the first white man's eyes that ever looked upon the Yosemite*" *above* the valley, and in that sense, he was certainly the original white discoverer.

Upon one occasion I told Capt. Walker that Ten-ie-ya had said that, "A small party of white men once crossed the mountains on the north side, but were so guided as not to see the valley proper." With a smile the captain said: "That was my party, but I was not deceived, for the lay of the land showed there was a valley below; but we had become nearly barefooted, our animals poor, and ourselves on the verge of starvation, so we followed down the ridge to Bull Creek, where, killing a deer, we went into camp."

All that I have ever claimed for myself is, that I was *one* of the party of white men who first *entered* the Yosemite Valley, as far as known to the Indians.

The fact of my naming the valley cannot be disputed. The existence of some terribly yawning abyss in the mountains, guarded at its entrance by a frightful "Rock Chief," from whose head rocks would be hurled down upon us if we attempted to enter that resort of demons, was frequently described to us by crafty or superstitious Indians. Hence the greater our surprise upon first beholding a fit abode for angels of light. As for myself, I freely confess that my feelings of hostility against the Indians were overcome by a sense of exaltation; and although I had suffered losses of property and friends, the natural right of the Indians to their inheritance forced itself upon my mind.

1850 IN THE SIERRA FOOTHILLS
BELOW THE YOSEMITE:
EVENTS LEADING TO WAR

The discovery of this remarkable region was an event intimately connected with the history of the early settlement of that portion of California. During 1850, the Indians in Mariposa county, which at that date included all the territory south of the divide of the Tuolumne and Merced rivers within the valley proper of the San Joaquin, became very troublesome to the miners and settlers. Their depredations and murderous assaults were continued until the arrival of the United States Indian commissioners, in 1851, when the general government assumed control over them. Through the management of the commissioners, treaties were made, and many of these Indians were transferred to locations reserved for their special occupancy.

It was in the early days of the operations of this commission that the Yosemite Valley was first entered by a command virtually employed to perform the special police duties of capturing and bringing the Indians before these representatives of the government, in order that treaties might be made with them. These wards of the general government were provided with supplies at the expense of the public treasury: provided that they confined themselves to the reservations selected for them.

My recollections of those early days are from personal observations and information derived from the earlier settlers of the San Joaquin Valley, with whom I was personally acquainted in the mining camps, and through business connections; and also from comrades in the Indian war of 1850-51. Among these settlers was one James D. Savage, a trader, who in 1849-50 was located in the mountains near the mouth of the South Fork of the Merced river, some fifteen miles below the Yosemite Valley.

At this point, engaged in gold mining, he had employed a party of native Indians. Early in the season of 1850 his trading post and mining camp were attacked by a band of the Yosemite Indians. This tribe, or band, claimed the territory in that vicinity, and attempted to drive Savage off. Their real object, however, was plunder. They were considered treacherous and dangerous, and were very troublesome to the miners generally.

Savage and his Indian miners repulsed the attack and drove off the marauders, but from this occurrence he no longer deemed this location desirable. Being fully aware of the murderous propensities of his assailants, he removed to Mariposa Creek, not far from the junction of the Aqua Fria, and near to the site of the old stone fort. Soon after, he established a branch post on the Fresno, where the mining prospects became most encouraging, as the high water subsided in that stream. This branch station was placed in charge of a man by the name of Greeley.

At these establishments Savage soon built up a prosperout business. He exchanged his goods at enormous profits for the gold obtained from his Indian miners.* The white miners and prospecting parties also submitted to his

*A can of oysters, five pounds of flour, or a pound of bacon cost an ounce of gold; a shirt required five ounces; a pair of boots or a hat went for a full pound! — editor.

demands rather than lose time by going to Mariposa village. The value of his patrons' time was thus made a source of revenue. As the season advanced, this hardy pioneer of commerce rapidly increased his wealth, but in the midst of renewed prosperity he learned that another cloud was gathering over him. One of his five squaws assured him that a combination was maturing among the mountain Indians, to kill or drive all the white men from the country, and plunder them of their property. To strengthen his influence over the principal tribes, Savage had, accord-

INDIAN SQUAWS GATHERING ROOTS AND BERRIES.

ing to the custom of many mountain men, taken wives from among them, supposing his personal safety would be somewhat improved by so doing. This is the old story of the prosperous Indian trader. Rumor also came from his Indian miners, that the Yosemites threatened to come down on him again for the purpose of plunder, and that they were urging other tribes to join them.

These reports he affected to disregard, but quietly cautioned the miners to guard against marauders.

He also sent word to the leading men in the settlements that hostilities were threatened, and advised preparations against a surprise.

At his trading posts he treated the rumors with indifference, but instructed the men in his employ to be continually on their guard in his absence. Stating that he was going to *"the Bay"* for a stock of goods, he started for San Francisco, taking with him two Indian wives, and a chief of some note and influence who professed great friendship.

This Indian, José Juarez, was in reality one of the leading spirits in arousing hostilities against the whites.

Notwithstanding Juarez appeared to show regard for Savage, the trader had doubts of his sincerity, but, as he had no fears of personal injury, he carefully kept his suspicions to himself. The real object Savage had in making this trip was to place in a safe locality a large amount of gold which he had on hand; and he took the chief to impress him with the futility of any attempted outbreak by his people. He hoped that a visit to Stockton and San Francisco, where José could see the numbers and superiority of the whites, would so impress him that on his return to the mountains his report would deter the Indians from their proposed hostilities.

The trip was made without any incidents of importance, but, to Savage's disappointment and regret, José developed an instinctive love for whiskey, and having been liberally supplied with gold, he invested heavily in that favorite Indian beverage, and was stupidly drunk nearly all the time he was in the city.

Becoming disgusted with José's frequent intoxication, Savage expressed in emphatic terms his disapprobation of such a course. José at once became greatly excited, and forgetting his usual reserve, retorted in abusive epithets, and disclosed his secret of the intended war against the whites.

Savage also lost his self-control, and with a blow felled the drunken Indian to the ground. José arose apparently sober, and from that time maintained a silent and dignified demeanor. After witnessing the celebration of the admission of the State into the Union—which by appointment occurred on October 29th, 1850, though the act of admission passed Congress on the 9th of September of that year— and making arrangements to have goods forwarded as he should order them, Savage started back with his dusky retainers for Mariposa. On his arrival at Quartzberg, he learned that the Kah-we-ah Indians were exacting tribute from the immigrants passing through their territory, and soon after his return a man by the name of Moore was killed not far from his Mariposa Station. From the information here received, and reported murders of emigrants, he scented danger to himself. Learning that the Indians were too numerous at "Cassady's Bar," on the San Joaquin, and in the vicinity of his Fresno Station, he at once, with characteristic promptness and courage, took his course direct to that post. He found, on arriving there, that all was quiet, although some Indians were about, as if for trading purposes. Among them were Pon-wat-chee and Vow-ches-ter, two Indian chiefs known to be friendly. The trader had taken two of his wives from their tribes.

Savage greeted all with his customary salutation. Leaving his squaws to confer with their friends and to provide for their own accommodations, he quietly examined the memoranda of his agent, and the supply of goods on hand. With an appearance of great indifference, he listened to the business reports and gossip of Greeley, who informed him that Indians from different tribes had come in but had brought but little gold. To assure himself of the progress made by the Indians in forming a union among themselves, he called those present around him in front of his store, and passed the friendly pipe. After the usual silence and delay, Savage said: "I know that all about me are my friends, and as a friend to all, I wish to have a talk with you before I go back to my home on the Mariposa, from which I have been a long distance away, but where I could not stop until I had warned you.

"I know that some of the Indians do not wish to be friends with the white men, and that they are trying to unite the different tribes for the purpose of a war. It is better for the Indians and white men to be friends. If the Indians make war on the white men, every tribe will be exterminated; not one will be left. I have just been where the white men are more numerous than the wasps and ants; and if war is made and the Americans are aroused to anger, every Indian engaged in the war will be killed before the whites will be satisfied." In a firm and impressive manner Savage laid before them the damaging effects of a war, and the advantages to all of a continued peaceful intercourse. His knowledge of Indian language was sufficient to make his remarks clearly understood, and they were apparently well received.

Not supposing that José would attempt there to advocate any of his schemes, the trader remarked, as he finished his speech: "A chief who has returned with me from the place where the white men are so numerous, can tell that what I have said is true—José Juarez—you all know, and will believe him when he tells you the white men are more powerful than the Indians.''

The cunning chief with much dignity, deliberately stepped forward, with more assurance than he had shown since the belligerent occurrence at the bay, and spoke with more energy than Savage had anticipated. He commenced by saying: ''Our brother has told his Indian relatives much that is truth; we have seen many people; the white men are very numerous; but the white men we saw on our visit are of many tribes; they are not like the tribe that dig gold in the mountains.'' He then gave an absurd description of what he had seen while below, and said: ''Those white tribes will not come to the mountains. They will not help the gold diggers if the Indians make war against them. If the gold diggers go to the white tribes in the big village they give their gold for strong water and games; when they have no more gold the white tribes drive the gold diggers back to the mountains with clubs. They strike them down (referring to the police), as your white relative struck me while I was with him.'' (His vindictive glance assured Savage that the blow was not forgotten or forgiven.) ''The white tribes will not go to war with the Indians in the mountains. They cannot bring their big ships and big guns to us; we have no cause to fear them. They will not injure us.''

To Savage's extreme surprise, he then boldly advocated an immediate war upon the whites, assuring his listeners that, as all the territory belonged to the Indians, if the tribes would unite the whole tribe of gold diggers could be easily driven from their country; but, if the gold diggers should stay longer, their numbers will be too great to make war upon, and the Indians would finally be destroyed. In his speech José evinced a keenness of observation inconsistent with his apparent drunken stupidity. Savage had thought this stupidity sometimes assumed. He now felt assured that the chief had expected thereby to learn his plans. To the writer there seems to be nothing inconsistent with Indian craft, keenness of observation and love of revenge in José's conduct, though he was frequently drunk while at "the bay." While José was speaking other Indians had joined the circle around him. Their expressions of approval indicated the effects of his speech. During this time Savage had been seated on a log in front of the store, a quiet listener. When José concluded, the trader arose, and stepping forward, calmly addressed the relatives of his wives and the Indians in whom he still felt confidence. The earnest and positive speech of the cunning chief had greatly surprised him; he was somewhat discouraged at the approval with which it had been received; but with great self-possession, he replied, "I have listened very attentively to what the chief, who went with me as my friend, has been saying to you. I have heard all he has said. He has told you of many things that he saw. He has told you some truth. He has told of many things which he knows nothing about. He has told you of things he saw in his dreams, while "strong water" made him sleep. The white men we saw there are all of the same tribe as the gold diggers here among the mountains. He has told you he saw white men that were pale, and had tall hats on their heads, with clothing different from the gold diggers. This was truth, but they are all brothers, all of one tribe. All can wear the clothing of the gold diggers; all can climb the mountains, and if war is made on the gold diggers, the white men will come and fight against the Indians. Their numbers will be so great, that every tribe will be destroyed that joins in a war against them."

José observing the effects of these statements, excitedly interrupted Savage by entering the circle, exclaiming: "He is telling you words that are not true. His tongue is forked and crooked. He is telling lies to his Indian relatives. This trader is not a friend to the Indians. He is not our brother. He will help the white gold diggers to drive the Indians from their country. We can now drive them from among us, and if the other white tribes should come to their help, we will go to the mountains; if they follow after us, they cannot find us; none of them will come back; we will kill them with arrows and with rocks." While José was thus vociferously haranguing, other Indians came into the grounds, and the crisis was approaching. As José Juarez ended his speech, José Rey, another influential chief and prominent leader, walked proudly into the now enlarged circle, followed by his suite of treacherous Chow-chillas, among whom were Tom-Kit and Frederico. He keenly glanced about him, and assuming a grandly tragic style, at once commenced a speech by saying: "My people are now ready to begin a war against the white gold diggers. If all the tribes will be as one tribe, and join with us, we will drive all the white men from our mountains. If all the tribes will go together, the white men will run from us, and leave their property behind them. The tribes who join in with my people will be the first to secure the property of the gold diggers."

The dignity and eloquent style of José Rey controlled the attention of the Indians. This appeal to their cupidity interested them; a common desire for plunder would be the strongest inducement to unite against the whites.

Savage was now fully aware that he had been defeated at this impromptu council he had himself organized, and at once withdrew to prepare for the hostilities he was sure would soon follow. As soon as the Indians dispersed, he started with his squaws for home, and again gave the settlers warning of what was threatened and would soon be attempted.

The reports from Savage were considered by the miners and settlers as absurd. It was generally known that mountain men of Savage's class were inclined to adopt the vagaries and superstitions of the Indians with whom they were associated; and therefore but little attention was given to the trader's warnings. It was believed that he had listened to the blatant palaver of a few vagabond "Digger Indians," and that the threatened hostilities were only a quarrel between Savage and his Indian miners, or with some of his Indian associates. Cassady, a rival trader, especially scoffed at the idea of danger, and took no precautions to guard himself or establishment. The settlers of Indian Gulch and Quartzberg were, however, soon after startled by a report brought by one of Savage's men called "Longhaired Brown," that the traders' store on the Fresno had been robbed, and all connected with it killed except himself.

Savage was highly offended at the indifference with which his cautions had been received at Mariposa, and by the county authorities, then located at Agua-Fria. He stated that his wives had assured him that a raid was about to be made on his establishment, and warned him of the danger of a surprise. He had at once sought aid from personal friends at Horse Shoe Bend—where he had once traded—to remove or protect his property. While he was absent, Greeley, Stiffner and Kennedy had been killed, his property plundered and burned, and his wives carried off by their own people. These squaws had been importuned to leave the trader, but had been faithful to his interests. The excitement of these occurrences had not subsided before news came of the murder of

Cassady and four men near the San Joaquin. Another murderous assault was soon after reported by an immigrant who arrived at Cassady's Bar, on the upper crossing of the San Joaquin. His shattered arm and panting horse excited the sympathies of the settlers, and aroused the whole community. The wounded man was provided for, and a party at once started for the "Four Creeks," where he had left his comrades fighting the Indians.

The arm of the wounded man was amputated by Dr. Lewis Leach, of St. Louis, Mo., an immigrant who had but just come in over the same route. The name of the wounded man was Frank W. Boden. He stated that his party—four men, I believe, besides himself—had halted at the "Four Creeks" to rest and graze their horses, and while there a band of Indians (Ka-we-ahs) came down from their village and demanded tribute for crossing their territory. Looking upon the demand as a new form of Indian beggary, but little attention was paid to them. After considerable bantering talk, some tobacco was given them, and they went off grumbling and threatening. Boden said: "After the Indians left we talked over the matter for a while; none regarded the demand of the 'Indian taxgathers' but as a trivial affair. I then mounted my horse and rode off in the direction in which we had seen some antelopes as we came on. I had not gone far before I heard firing in the direction of our halting-place.

"Riding back, I saw the house near which I had left my comrades was surrounded by yelling demons. I was discovered by them at the same instant, and some of them dashed toward me. Seeing no possibility of joining my party, I turned and struck my horse with the spurs, but before I could get beyond range of their arrows, I felt a benumbing sensation in my arm, which dropped powerless. Seeing that my arm was shattered or broken, I thought I would give them one shot at least before I fell into their hands. Checking my horse with some difficulty, I turned so as to rest my rifle across my broken arm, and took sight on the nearest of my pursuers, who halted at the same time.''

At this point in his story the hardy adventurer remarked with a twinkle of satisfaction in his bright, keen eye: ''I never took better aim in my life. That Indian died suddenly. Another dash was made for me. My horse did not now need the spurs, he seemed to be aware that we must leave that locality as soon as possible, and speedily distanced them all. As soon as the first excitement was over I suffered excruciating pain in my arm. My rifle being useless to me, I broke it against a tree and threw it away. I then took the bridle rein in my teeth and carried the broken arm in my other hand.''

The party that went out to the place of attack—Dr. Thomas Payn's, now Visalia, named for Nat. Vice, an acquaintance of the writer—found there the mangled bodies of Boden's four companions. One of these, it was shown by unmistakable evidence, had been skinned by the merciless fiends while yet alive.

It now became necessary that some prompt action should be taken for general protection. Rumors of other depredations and murders alarmed the inhabitants of Mariposa county. Authentic statements of these events were at once forwarded to Governor John McDougal, by the sheriff and other officials, and citizens, urging the immediate adoption of some measures on the part of the State for the defense of the people. Raids upon the miners' camps and the "Ranch" of the settlers had become so frequent that on its being rumored that the Indians were concentrating for more extensive operations, a party, without waiting for any official authority, collected and started out to check the ravages of the marauders that were found gathering among the foothills. With but limited supplies, and almost without organization, this party made a rapid and toilsome march among the densely wooded mountains in pursuit of the savages, who, upon report of our movements, were now retreating. This party came up with the Indians at a point high up on the Fresno. In the skirmish which followed a Lt. Skeane was killed, William Little was seriously wounded and some others slightly injured.

This engagement, which occurred on January 11th, 1851, was not a very satisfactory one to the whites. The necessity of a more efficient organization was shown.

The leaders in exciting hostilities against the whites were José Juarez and José Rey. The bands collected on this mountain were under the leadership of José Rey, who was also known by his English name of "King Joseph." The tribes represented were the Chow-chilla, Chook-chancie, Noot-chu, Ho-nah-chee, Po-to-en-cie, Po-ho-no-chee, Kah-we-ah and Yosemite. The number of fighting men or warriors was estimated at about 500, while that of the whites did not exceed 100.

It was late in the day when the Indians were discovered.

The plan was that an attack should be undertaken at daylight, and that an effort should be made to set fire to the village, preliminary to the general assault. This plan was strongly advocated by the more experienced ones who had seen service in Mexico and in Indian warfare.

But thirty-six men were detached for the preliminary service. Everything being arranged the attacking party started before daylight. Without the least delay the men dashed in and with brands from the camp fires, set the wigwams burning, and at the same time madly attacked the now alarmed camp. The light combustible materials of which the wigwams were composed were soon in a bright blaze. So rapid and so sudden were the charges made, that the panic-stricken warriors at once fled from their stronghold. José Rey was among the first shot down.

The whole camp was routed, and sought safety among the rocks and brush. No prisoners were taken; twenty-three were killed; the number wounded was never known. Of the settlers, but one was really wounded, though several were scorched and bruised in the fight. None were killed.

THE State authorities had in the meantime become aroused. The reports of Indian depredations multiplied, and a general uprising was for a time threatened.

Proclamations were therefore issued by Gov. McDougal, calling for volunteers, to prevent further outrages and to punish the marauders. Our impromptu organization formed the nucleus of the volunteer force in Mariposa county, as a large majority of the men at once enlisted.

Our new organization, when full, numbered two hundred mounted men.

THE MARIPOSA BATTALION: Muster-in

The date from which we were regularly mustered into the service was January 24th, 1851. The volunteers provided their own horses and equipments. The camp supplies and baggage trains were furnished by the State. This military force was called into existence by the State authorities, but by act of Congress its maintenance was at the expense of the general government, under direction of Indian commissioners.

The officers, chosen by the men, recommended to and commissioned by Governor McDougal, were James D. Savage, as Major; John J. Kuy-ken-dall, John Boling, and William Dill, as Captains; M. B. Lewis, as Adjutant; John I. Scott, Reuben T. Chandler, and Hugh W. Farrell, as First Lieutenants; Robert E. Russell, as Sergeant Major; Dr. A. Bronson, as Surgeon, and Drs. Pfifer and Black as Assistant Surgeons. A few changes of Lieutenants and subordinate officers were afterward made.

The attack made upon Savage on the Merced river in 1850 had for its object plunder and intimidation, and as an invasion of Ten-ie-ya's territory was no longer threatened after the removal of Mr. Savage to the Mariposa, the Yo Semites contented themselves with the theft of horses and clothing, but a general war was still impending, as may be seen by reference to page 31 of "In The Heart of The Sierras," where appears: Report of Col. Adam Johnston, a special agent, to Gov. Peter H. Burnett, upon his return from Mariposa county to San José, then the Capital of California, and which I here present: San José, January 2, 1851. Sir: I have the honor to submit to you, as the executive of the State of California, some facts connected with the recent depredations committed by the Indians, within the bounds of the State, upon the persons and property of her citizens. The immediate scene of their hostile movements are at and in the vicinity of the Mariposa and Fresno. Accordingly...

Friday, the 20th, I left the Mariposa camp with thirty-five men, for the camp on the Fresno. It presented a horrid scene of savage cruelty. The Indians had destroyed everything they could not use or carry with them. The store was stripped of blankets, clothing, flour, and everything of value; the safe was broken open and rifled of its contents; the cattle, horses and mules had been run into the mountains; the murdered men had been stripped of their clothing, and lay before us filled with arrows; one of them had yet twenty perfect arrows sticking in him.

The report of Col. Johnston to Gov. Burnett had the desired result, for immediately after inauguration, his successor, Gov. McDougal, on January 13, 1851, issued a proclamation calling for one hundred volunteers, and this number by a subsequent order dated January 24th, 1851, after receipt of Sheriff James Burney's report, bearing the same date of the Governor's first call for one hundred men, was increased to "two hundred able-bodied men, under officers of their own selection."

But we have now the report of Major Burney to Gov. McDougal:

AGUA FRIA, January 13, 1851.

SIR: Your Excellency has doubtlessly been informed by Mr. Johnston and others, of repeated and aggravated depredations of the Indians in this part of the State. Their more recent outrages you are probably not aware of.

Since the departure of Mr. Johnston, the Indian agent, they have killed a portion of the citizens on the head of the San Joaquin river, driven the balance off, taken away all movable property, and destroyed all they could not take away. They have invariably murdered and robbed all the small parties they fell in with between here and the San Joaquin. News came here last night that seventy-two men were killed on Rattlesnake creek; several men have been killed in Bear Valley. The Fine Gold Gulch has been deserted, and the men came in here yesterday. Nearly all the mules and horses in this part of the State have been stolen, both from the mines and the ranches. And I now, in the name of the people of this part of the State, and for the good of our country, appeal to Your Excellency for assistance.

The Mariposa Battalion was assigned by Governor Mc-Dougal to the duty of keeping in subjection the Indian tribes on the east side of the San Joaquin and Tulare valleys, from the Tuolumne river to the Te-hon Pass. As soon as the battalion was organized, Major Savage began his preparations for an expedition. There was but little delay in fitting out. Scouting parties were sent out, but with no other effect than to cause a general retreat of the Indians to the mountains, and a cessation of hostilities, except the annoyances from the small bands of thieving marauders. No Indians were overtaken by those detachments, though they were often seen provokingly near. When about to start on a more extended expedition to the mountains, Major Savage received an order from the Governor to suspend hostile operations until he should receive further instructions. We learned at about the same time through the newspapers, as well as from the Governor's messenger, that the United States Commissioners had arrived in San Francisco. Their arrival had for some time been expected.

Up to this period the Indian affairs of California had not been officially administered upon. Public officers had not before been appointed to look after the vast landed estates of the aboriginal proprietors of this territory, and to provide for their heirs. After some delay, the commissioners arrived at our camp, which was located about fifteen miles below Mariposa village. Here the grazing was most excellent, and for that reason they temporarily established their headquarters. These officials were Colonels Barbour and McKee, and Dr. Woozencroft. They were accompanied by Col. Neely Johnson, the Governor's aid, and by a small detachment of regulars. The commissioners at once proceeded to make a thorough investigation into the cause of the war, and of the condition of affairs generally. Having secured the services of some of the Mission Indians, these were sent out with instructions to notify all the tribes that the commissioners had been directed by the President to make peace between them and the white settlers; and that if they would come in, they should be assured protection.

The so-called Mission Indians were members of different tribes who had been instructed in the belief of the Catholic Church, at the old Spanish missions. These Indians had not generally taken part in the war against the white settlers, although some of them, with the hostiles, were the most treacherous of their race, having acquired the vices and none of the virtues of their white instructors.

During this period of preliminaries a few Indians ventured in to have a talk with the commissioners. They were very shy and suspicious, for all had been more or less implicated in the depredations that had been committed. Presents were lavishly distributed, and assurances were given that all who came in should be supplied with food and clothing and other useful things. This policy soon became generally known to the Indians.

Among the delegations that visited the commissioners were Vow-ches-ter,* chief of one of the more peaceful bands, and Russio, a Mission Indian from the Tuolumne, but who in former years had belonged to some of the San Joaquin tribes. These chiefs had always appeared friendly, and had not joined in the hostile attitude assumed by the others. At the outbreak on the Fresno, Vow-ches-ter had been temporarily forced into hostilities by the powerful influence of José Rey, and by his desire to secure protection to his relative, one of Savage's squaws. But with the fall of José Rey, his influence over Vow-ches-ter declined, and he was once more left free to show his friendship for the whites. As for Russio, his intelligent services were secured as peacemaker and general Indian interpreter by the commissioners, while a much less competent Mission Indian, Sandino, served in the capacity of interpreter during expeditions into the mountains.

Having been assured of safety, these two chiefs promised to bring in their people and make peace with the whites. All that came in promised a cessation, on the part of their tribes, of the hostilities begun, for which they were rewarded with presents.

Vow-ches-ter, when questioned, stated "that the mountain tribes would not listen to any terms of peace involving the abandonment of their territory; that in the fight near the North Fork of the San Joaquin, José Rey had been badly wounded and probably would die; that his tribe were very angry, and would not make peace." We had up to this time supposed José Rey had been killed at "Battle Mountain." Russio said: "The Indians in the deep rocky valley on the Merced river do not wish for peace, and will not come in to see the chiefs sent by the great father to make treaties. They think the white men cannot find their

---

*An Indian corruption of Bautista.

hiding places, and that therefore they cannot be driven out.'' The other Indians of the party confirmed Russio's statements. Vow-ches-ter was the principal spokesman, and he said: ''In this deep valley spoken of by Russio, one Indian is more than ten white men. The hiding places are many. They will throw rocks down on the white men, if any should come near them. The other tribes dare not make war upon them, for they are lawless like the grizzlies, and as strong. We are afraid to go to this valley, for there are many witches there.''

Some of us did not consider Vow-ches-ter's promise of friendship as reliable. We regarded him as one of the hostile mountain Indians. He, however, was never again engaged in hostilities against the whites. I afterwards learned that Vow-ches-ter and Savage had once professed a strong friendship for each other. The trader at that time had taken a bride who was closely allied to the chief. After the destruction of Savage's trading posts, in which Vow-ches-ter had taken an active part in procuring a forcible divorce and division of property (though the murders were ascribed to the Chow-chillas), all forms of friendship or relationship had ceased. At this interview no sign of recognition passed. After listening to this parley between the commissioners and the Indians, I asked Major Savage, who had been acting as interpreter, if he had ever been into the deep valley the Indians had been speaking of. He at first replied that he had, but on a subsequent conversation he corrected this statement by saying, ''Last year while I was located at the mouth of the South Fork of the Merced, I was attacked by the Yosemites, but with the Indian miners I had in my employ, drove them off, and followed some of them up the Merced river into a cañon, which I supposed led to their stronghold, as the Indians then with me said it was not a safe place to go into. From the appearance of this rocky gorge I had no difficulty in believing them. Fearing an ambush, I did not follow them. It was on this account that I changed my location to Mariposa creek. I would like to get into the den of the thieving murderers. If ever I have a chance I will smoke out the Grizzly Bears (the Yosemites) from their holes, where they are thought to be so secure.''

No peace messengers came in from the mountain Indians, who continued to annoy the settlers with their depredations, thieving from the miners' camps, and stealing horses and mules from the ranches. While we were awaiting the action of the commissioners, we lost some horses and mules, which were stolen from the vicinity of our camp. After the commissioners had decided upon the measures to be adopted, our battalion was ordered into line and we were then officially informed by Col. Johnson, that our operations as a military organization would henceforth be under the direction of the United States Commissioners. That by their order we were now assigned to the duty of subduing such Indian tribes as could not otherwise be induced to make treaties with them, and at once cease hostilities and depredations. ''Your officers will make all reports to the commissioners. Your orders and instructions will hereafter be issued by them.'' The colonel then complimented the soldierly appearance of the battalion (very customary in later years) and then said: ''While I do not hesitate to denounce the Indians for the murders and robberies committed by them, we should not forget that there may perhaps be circumstances which, if taken into consideration, might to some extent excuse their hostility to the whites. They probably feel that they themselves are the aggrieved party, looking upon us as trespassers upon their territory, invaders of their country, and seeking to dispossess them of their homes. It may be, they class us with the Spanish invaders of Mexico and California, whose cruelties in civil-izing and Christianizing them are still traditionally fresh in their memories," etc. In conclusion the colonel said: "As I am about to leave, I will now bid you 'good-bye,' with the hope that your actions will be in harmony with the wishes of the commissioners, and that in the performance of your duties, you will in all cases observe mercy where severity is not justly demanded."

Colonel Johnson gave us a very excellent little speech; but at that time we were not fully impressed with the just-ness of the remarks which had been made from kindness of heart and sincerely humane feelings. Many of us had lost—some heavily—by the depredations of the Indians. Friends and relatives had been victims of their atrocities. Murders and robberies had been committed without provo-cations then discernible to us. Many of us would then have been willing to adopt the methods of the old Spanish mis-sionaries, who, it was said, sometimes brought in their con-verts with the lasso. However, these orders and the speech from Col. Johnson were received with cheers by the more impatient and impulsive of the volunteers, who preferred active service to the comparative quiet of the camp.

The commissioners selected a reservation on the Fresno, near the foothills, about eighteen or twenty miles from our camp, to which the Indian tribes with whom treaties had been made were to be removed, and at this locality the commissioners also established a camp, as headquarters.

The deliberative action on the part of the commissioners, who were very desirous of having the Indians voluntarily come in to make treaties with them, delayed any active co-operation on the part of our battalion until the winter rains had fully set in. Our first extended expedition to the mountains was made during the prevailing storms of the vernal equinox, although detachments had previously made excursions into the country bordering upon the Sierras. This region, like parts of Virginia, proved impassable to a mounted force during the wet season, and our operations were confined to a limited area.

INDIANS GATHERING NUTS OF THE DIGGER-PINE.

FALLS OF TA-SA-YVE, BY THOMAS AYRES, 1855 OR 1856

UP TO THE MOUNTAINS:
FIRST SURRENDER OF THE YOSEMITES

It was at last decided that more extended operations were necessary to bring in the mountain tribes. Although there was no longer unity of action among them, they refused to leave their retreats, and had become even suspicious of each other. The defeat of José Rey, and the desertion of the tribes who had made, or had promised to make, treaties with the commissioners, and had ceased from all hostile demonstrations, had caused jealousies and discontent to divide even the most turbulent bands. For the extended operations of the battalion among the mountains, it was decided that Major Savage, with the companies of Captains Boling and Dill, should make expeditions which would require him to traverse the regions of the San Joaquin and Merced rivers. Captain Kuy-ken-dall with his company were to be detached to operate for the same purpose in the regions of the Kings and Kah-we-ah rivers. The Indians captured were to be escorted to the commissioners' camp on the Fresno. Notwithstanding a storm was gathering, our preparations were cheerfully made, and when the order to "form into line" was given, it was obeyed with alacrity. No "bugle call" announced orders to us; the "details" were made quietly, and we as quietly assembled. Promptly as the word of command "mount," was given, every saddle was filled. With "forward march," we naturally filed off into the order of march so readily assumed by mounted frontiersmen while traveling on a trail.

We left our camp as quietly and as orderly as such an undisciplined body could be expected to move, but Major Savage said that we must all learn to be as still as Indians, or we would never find them.

This battalion was a body of hardy, resolute pioneers. Many of them had seen service, and had fought their way against the Indians across the plains; some had served in the war with Mexico and been under military discipline.

Although ununiformed, they were well armed, and their similarities of dress and accoutrements gave them a general military appearance.

The temperature was mild and agreeable at our camp near the plain, but we began to encounter storms of cold rain as we reached the more elevated localities.

Major Savage being aware that rain on the foothills and plain at that season of the year indicated snow higher up, sent forward scouts to intercept such parties as might attempt to escape, but the storm continued to rage with such violence as to render this order useless, and we found the scouts awaiting us at the foot of a mountain known as the Black Ridge. This ridge is a spur of the Sierra Nevadas. It separates the Mariposa, Chow-chilla, Fresno and San Joaquin rivers on the south from the Merced on the north. While halting for a rest, and sipping his coffee, Savage expressed an earnest desire to capture the village he had ascertained to be located over the ridge on the South Fork of the Merced. He was of the opinion that if it could be reached without their discovery of us, we should have no fighting to do there, as that band would surrender at once rather than endanger their women and children, who would be unable to escape through the snow. Toward this village we therefore marched as rapidly as the nature of the steep and snow-obstructed trail would permit us to travel. An Indian that answered to the name of ''Bob,'' an *attache* of the Major, serving as guide. Climbing up this steep black mountain, we soon reached the region of snow, which at the summit was fully four feet deep, though the cold was not intense. By this time night was upon us.

The trail led over the ridge at a point where its tabled summit was wooded with a forest of pines, cedars and firs, so dense as almost to exclude the light of the stars that now and then appeared struggling through the gloom.

We laboriously followed our guide and file leader, but this trail was so indistinctly seen in the darkness, that at intervals deep mutterings would be heard from some drowsy rider who missed the beaten path. As we commenced the descent of the ridge, the expressions became more forcible than polite when some unlucky ones found themselves floundering in the snow below the uncertain trail. If left to their own sagacity, a horse or mule will follow its leader; but if a self-willed rider insists upon his own judgment, the poor animal has not only to suffer the extra fatigue incurred by a misstep, but also the punishment of the spur, and hear the explosive maledictions of the master. The irritating responses of his comrades that "another fool has been discovered," was not then calculated to sooth the wrath that was then let loose.

With short halts and repeated burrowings in the deep, damp snow, the South Fork of the Merced was at length reached about a mile below what is now known as Clark's, or Wah-wo-na, from Wah-ha wo-na, a Big Tree. We here made a halt, and our weary animals were provided with some barley, for the snow was here over a foot deep. The major announced that it was but a short distance below to the Indian village, and called for volunteers to accompany him—it might be for a fight or perhaps only a footrace—circumstances would determine which. The major's call was promptly and fully answered, although all were much fatigued with the tedious night march. The animals were left, and a sufficient number was selected to remain as a reserve force and camp guard. At daylight we filed away on foot to our destination, following the major who was guided by "Bob."

THERE was a very passable trail for horses leading down the right bank of the river, but it was overlooked on the left bank by the Indian village, which was situated on a high point at a curve in the river that commanded an extensive view up and down. To avoid being seen, the major led us along down the left bank, where we were compelled, at times, to wade into the rushing torrent to avoid the precipitous and slippery rocks, which, in places, dipped into the stream. Occasionally, from a stumble, or from the deceptive depths of the clear mountain stream, an unfortunate one was immersed in the icy fluid, which seemed colder than the snow-baths of the mountain. With every precaution, some became victims to these mischances, and gave vent to their emotions, when suddenly immersed, by hoarse curses, which could be heard above the splash and roar of the noisy water. These men (headed by Surgeon Bronson) chilled and benumbed, were sent back to the camp to "dry their ammunition."(?) After passing this locality— our march thus far having alternated in snow and water— we arrived, without being discovered, in sight of the smoke of their camp-fires, where we halted for a short rest.

On the arrival of Captains Boling and Dill with their respective companies, we were deployed into skirmish line, and advanced toward the encampment without any effort at concealment. On discovering us the Indians hurriedly ran to and fro, as if uncertain what course to pursue. Seeing an unknown force approaching, they threw up their hands in token of submission, crying out at the same time in Spanish, *"Pace! pace!"* (peace! peace!) We were at once ordered to halt while Major Savage went forward to arrange for the surrender. The major was at once recognized and cordially received by such of the band as he desired to confer with officially. We found the village to be that of Pon-wat-chee, a chief of the Noot-chü tribe, whose people had formerly worked for Savage under direction of Cow-chit-ty, his brother, and from whose tribe Savage had taken Ee-e-ke-no, one of his former wives. The chief professed still to entertain feelings of friendship for Savage, saying that he was now willing to obey his counsels. Savage, in response, lost no time in preliminary affairs.

He at once told the chief the object of the expedition, and his requirements. His terms were promptly agreed to, and before we had time to examine the captives or their wigwams, they had commenced packing their supplies and removing their property from their bark huts. This done, the torch was applied by the Indians themselves, in token of their sincerity in removing to the reservations on the Fresno.

By the major's orders they had at once commenced their preparations for removal to a rendezvous, which he had selected nearly opposite this encampment, which was accessible to horses. This plateau was also the location designated for our camp. This camp was afterwards used by an employé at the agency, whose name was Bishop, and was known as Bishop's Camp. It is situated on an elevated table, on the right side of the valley of the South Fork.

While the Indians were preparing for their transfer to the place selected, our tired and hungry men began to feel the need of rest and refreshments. We had traveled a much longer distance since the morning before than had been estimated in expectation of a halt, and many of the men had not tasted food since the day before.

John Hankin told Major Savage that if a roast dog could be procured, he would esteem it an especial favor. Bob McKee thought this a capital time to learn to eat acorn bread, but after trying some set before him by "a young

INDIAN SQUAW AND PAPOOSE.

and accomplished squaw," as the major cynically termed her, concluded he was not yet hungry enough for its enjoyment.

A call was made for volunteers to go back to bring up the reserve and supplies, but the service was not very promptly accepted. McKee, myself and two others, however, offered to go with the order to move down to the selected rendezvous. Three Indians volunteered to go with us as guides; one will seldom serve alone. We found the trail on the right bank less laborious to travel than was expected, for the snow had mostly disappeared from the loose, sandy soil, which upon this side of the river has a southwesterly exposure. On our arrival in camp preparations were begun to obey the order of the major. While coffee was being prepared Doctor Bronson wisely prescribed and most skillfully administered to us a refreshing draught of "*Aqua Ardente.*"

After a hasty *breakfast,* we took to our saddles, and taking a supply of biscuits and cold meat, left the train and arrived at the new camp ground just as our hungry comrades came up from the Indian village. The scanty supplies, carried on our saddles, were thankfully received and speedily disposed of. The Indians had not yet crossed the river. We found that we had traveled about twelve miles, while our comrades and the captives had accomplished only three.

From this camp, established as our headquarters, or as a base of operations while in this vicinity, Major Savage sent Indian runners to the bands who were supposed to be hiding in the mountains. These messengers were instructed to assure all the Indians that if they would go and make treaties with the commissioners, they would there be furnished with food and clothing, and receive protection, but if they did not come in, he should make war upon them until he destroyed them all.

Pon-wat-chee had told the major when his own village was captured, that a small band of Po-ho-no-chees were encamped on the sunny slope of the divide of the Merced, and he having at once dispatched a runner to them, they began to come into camp. This circumstance afforded encouragement to the major, but Pon-wat-chee was not entirely sanguine of success with the Yosemites, though he told the major that if the snow continued deep they could not escape.

At first but few Indians came in, and these were very cautious—dodging behind rocks and trees, as if fearful we would not recognize their friendly signals.

Being fully assured by those who had already come in, of friendly treatment, all soon came in who were in our immediate vicinity. None of the Yosemites had responded to the general message sent. Upon a special envoy being sent to the chief, he appeared the next day in person. He came alone, and stood in dignified silence before one of the guard, until motioned to enter camp. He was immediately recognized by Pon-wat-chee as Ten-ie-ya, the old chief of the Yosemites, and was kindly cared for—being well supplied with food—after which, with the aid of the other Indians, the major informed him of the wishes of the commissioners. The old sachem was very suspicious of Savage, and feared he was taking this method of getting the Yosemites into his power for the purpose of revenging his personal wrongs. Savage told him that if he would go to the commissioners and make a treaty of peace with them, as the other Indians were going to do, there would be no more war. Ten-ie-ya cautiously inquired as to the object of taking all the Indians to the plains of the San Joaquin Valley, and said: "My people do not want anything from the 'Great Father' you tell me about. The Great Spirit is our father, and he has always supplied us with all we need. We do not want anything from white men. Our women are able to do our work. Go, then; let us remain in the mountains where we were born; where the ashes of our fathers have been given to the winds. I have said enough!''

This was abruptly answered by Savage, in Indian dialect and gestures: ''If you and your people have all you desire, why do you steal our horses and mules? Why do you rob the miners' camps? Why do you murder the white men, and plunder and burn their houses?''

Ten-ie-ya sat silent for some time; it was evident he understood what Savage had said, for he replied: ''My young men have sometimes taken horses and mules from the whites. It was wrong for them to do so. It is not wrong to take the property of enemies, who have wronged my people. My young men believed the white gold-diggers were our enemies; we now know they are not, and we will be glad to live in peace with them. We will stay here and be friends. My people do not want to go to the plains. The tribes who go there are some of them very bad. They will make war on my people. We cannot live on the plains with them. Here we can defend ourselves against them.''

In reply to this Savage very deliberately and firmly said: ''Your people must go to the commissioners and make terms with them. If they do not, your young men will again steal our horses, your people will again kill and plunder the whites. It was your people who robbed my stores, burned my houses, and murdered my men. If they do not make a treaty, your whole tribe will be destroyed, not one of them will be left alive.'' At this vigorous ending of the major's speech, the old chief replied: ''It is useless to talk to you about who destroyed your property and killed your people. If the Chow-chillas do not boast of it, they are cowards, for they led us on. I am old and you can kill me if you will, but what use to lie to you who know more than all the Indians, and can beat them in their big hunts of deer and bear. Therefore I will not lie to you, but promise that if allowed to return to my people I will bring them in." He was allowed to go. The next day he came back, and said his people would soon come to our camp; that when he had told them they could come with safety they were willing to go and make a treaty with the men sent by the "Great Father," who was so good and rich. Another day passed, but no Indians made their appearance from the "deep valley," spoken of so frequently by those at our camp. The old chief said the snow was so deep that they could not travel fast, that his village was so far down (gesticulating, by way of illustration, with his hands) that when the snow was deep on the mountains they would be a long time climbing out of it. As we were at the time having another storm Ten-ie-ya's explanation was accepted, but was closely watched.

The next day passed without their coming, although the snowstorm had ceased during the night before. It was then decided that it would be necessary to go to the village of the Yosemites, and bring them in; and in case they could not be found there, to follow to their hiding-places in the deep cañon, so often represented as such a dangerous locality. Ten-ie-ya was questioned as to the route and the time it would take his people to come in; and when he learned we were going to his village, he represented that the snow was so deep that the horses could not go through it. He also stated that the rocks were so steep that our horses could not climb out of the valley if they should go into it. Captain Boling caused Ten-ie-ya's statements to be made known to his men. It was customary in all of our expeditions where the force was divided, to call for volunteers. The men were accordingly drawn up into line, and the call made that all who wished to go to the village of the Yosemites were to step three paces to the front. When the order to advance was given, to the surprise of Captains Boling and Dill, each company moved in line as if on parade. The entire body had volunteered. As a camp-guard was necessary, a call was then made for volunteers for this duty. When the word "march" was again repeated, but a limited number stepped to the front. Captain Boling, with a smile on his good-natured face, said: "A camp-guard will have to be provided in some way. I honor the sentiment that prompted you all to volunteer for the exploration, and I also appreciate the sacrifice made by those who are willing to stay; but these are too few. Our baggage, supplies and Indian captives must be well guarded. I endeavored to make the choice of duty voluntary, by representing the difficulties that might reasonably be expected, and thus secure those best suited for the respective duty of field and camp. I am baffled, but not defeated, for I have another test of your fitness; it is a foot-race. You know it has been represented to us by Ten-ie-ya that the route to his village is an extremely difficult one, and impassable for our horses. It may not be true, but it will be prudent to select men for the expedition who have proved their endurance and fleetness. I now propose that you decide what I have found so difficult."

This proposition was received with shouts of laughter, and the arrangements for the contest were at once commenced, as it afforded a source of frolicsome amusement. A hundred yards were paced off, and the goal conspicuously marked. A distance line was to determine who should constitute the camp-guard. I doubt if such boisterous hilarity and almost boyish merriment was ever before seen while making a detail from any military organization.

The Indians were at first somewhat alarmed at the noisy preparations, and began to be fearful of their safety, but on learning the cause of the excitement they, too, became interested in the proceedings, and expressed a desire to participate in the race. Two or three were allowed to join in as proxies for the *"heavy ones"* who concluded not to run, though willing to pay the young Indians to represent them in the race, provided they came out ahead. One young Indian did beat every man, except Bob McKee, for whom he manifested great admiration. Many anxious ones ran barefooted in the snow. The Indian's motions were not impeded by any civilized garments; a modest waist cloth was all they had on. In subsequent races, after a long rest, several of our men demonstrated that their racing powers were superior to the fastest of the Indian runners. Captain Boling's racing scheme brought out the strong points of the runners. Enough were distanced in both companies to secure an ample camp-guard. The envious guard raised the point that this method of detail was simply a proof of legs, not brains. It was reported in camp that Captain Boling had kept a record of the speedy ones which he had filed away for future use in cases where fleetness of foot would be required for extra duties.

Preparations were made for an early start the next morning. The officer to be left in charge of the camp was instructed to allow the Indians all liberty consistent with *safety,* and to exercise no personal restraint over them unless there should be an evident attempt to leave in a body; when, of course, any movement of the kind was to be defeated. The major said: "I deem the presence of the women and children a sufficient hostage for the peaceful conduct of the men, but do not allow *any of them* to enter our tents, or we may lose possession."

As no information had been received from the camp of the Yosemites, after an early breakfast, the order was passed to "fall in," and when the order "march" was

INDIAN SQUAWS GATHERING PINE CONES

given, we moved off in single file, Savage leading, with Ten-ie-ya as guide.

From the length of time taken by the chief to go and return from his encampment, it was supposed that with horses, and an early start, we should be able to go and return the same day, if for any cause it should be deemed desirable, although sufficient supplies were taken, in case of a longer delay.

While ascending to the divide between the South Fork and the main Merced we found but little snow, but at the divide, and beyond, it was from three to five feet in depth, and in places much deeper. The sight of this somewhat cooled our ardor, but none asked for a *"furlough."*

To somewhat equalize the laborious duties of making a trail, each man was required to take his turn in front. The leader of the column was frequently changed; no horse or mule could long endure the fatigue without relief. To effect this, the tired leader dropped out of line, resigning his position to his followers, taking a place in the rear, on the beaten trail, exemplifying, that "the first shall be last, and the last shall be first." The snow packed readily, so that a very comfortable trail was left in the rear of our column.

Old Ten-ie-ya relaxed the rigidity of his bronze features, in admiration of our method of making a trail, and assured us that, notwithstanding the depth of snow, we would soon reach his village. We had in our imaginations pictured it as in some deep, rocky cañon in the mountains.

While in camp the frantic efforts of the old chief to describe the location to Major Savage had resulted in the unanimous verdict among the "boys," who were observing him, that "it must be a devil of a place." Feeling encouraged by the hope that we should soon arrive at the residences of his Satanic majesty's subjects, we wallowed on, alternately becoming the object of a joke, as we in turn were extricated from the drifts. When we had traversed a little more than half the distance, as was afterwards proved, we met the Yosemites on their way to our rendezvous on the South Fork.

As they filed past us, the major took account of their number, which was but seventy-two. As they reached our beaten trail, satisfaction was variously expressed, by grunts from the men, by the low rippling laughter from the squaws, and by the children clapping their hands in glee at the sight. On being asked where the others of his band were, the old sachem said: "This is all of my people that are willing to go with me to the plains. Many that have been with me are from other tribes. They have taken wives from my band; all have gone with their wives and children to the Tuolumne and to the Monos." Savage told Ten-ie-ya that he was telling him that which was not true. The Indians could not cross the mountains in the deep snow, neither could they go over the divide of the Tuolumne. That he knew they were still at his village or in hiding places near it. Ten-ie-ya assured the major he was telling him the truth, and in a very solemn manner declared that none of his band had been left behind—that all had gone before his people had left. His people had not started before because of the snowstorm.

With a belief that but a small part of Ten-ie-ya's band was with this party, Major Savage decided to go on to the Indian village and ascertain if any others could be found or traces of them discovered. This decision was a satisfactory one and met with a hearty approval as it was reported along the line.

This tribe had been estimated by Pon-wat-chee and Cow-chit-tee as numbering more than two hundred; as about that number usually congregated when they met together to "*cache*" their acorns in the valley, or for a grand annual hunt and drive of game; a custom which secured an abundant supply for the feast that followed.

At other times they were scattered in bands on the sunny slopes of the ridges, and in the mountain glens. Ten-ie-ya had been an unwilling guide thus far, and Major Savage said to him. "You may return to camp with your people, and I will take one of your young men with me. There are but few of your people here. Your tribe is large. I am going to your village to see your people, who will not come with you. They *will* come with me if I find them."

Savage then selected one of the young "braves" to accompany him. Ten-ie-ya replied, as the young Indian stepped forward by his direction, "I will go with my people; my young man shall go with you to my village. You will not find any people there. I do not know where they are. My tribe is small—not large, as the white chief has said. The Pai-utes and Monos are all gone. Many of the people with my tribe are from western tribes that have come to me and do not wish to return. If they go to the plains and are seen, they will be killed by the friends of those with whom they had quarreled. I have talked with my people and told them I was going to see the white chiefs sent to make peace. I was told that I was growing old, and it was well that I should go, but that young and strong men can find plenty in the mountains; therefore why should they go? to be yarded like horses and cattle. My heart has been sore since that talk, but I am now willing to go, for it is best for my people that I do so."

The major listened to the old Indian's volubility for awhile, but interrupted him with a cheering "Forward march!" at which the impatient command moved briskly forward over the now partly broken trail, leaving the chief alone, as his people had already gone on.

"THE DOMES OF THE YOSEMITE", THOMAS AYRES, 1855

INTO THE YOSEMITE: MARCH 25, 1851

We found the traveling much less laborious than before, and it seemed but a short time after we left the Indians before we suddenly came in full view of the valley in which was the village, or rather the encampments of the Yosemites. The immensity of rock I had seen in my vision on the Old Bear Valley trail from Ridley's Ferry was here presented to my astonished gaze. The mystery of that scene was here disclosed. My awe was increased by this nearer view. The face of the immense cliff was shadowed by the declining sun; its outlines only had been seen at a distance. This towering mass

> "Fools our fond gaze, and greatest of the great,
> Defies at first our Nature's littleness,
> Till, growing with (to) its growth, we thus dilate
> Our spirits to the size of that they contemplate."

That stupendous cliff is now known as "El Capitan" (the Captain), and the plateau from which we had our first view of the valley, as Mount Beatitude.

It has been said that "it is not easy to describe in words the precise impressions which great objects make upon us." I cannot describe how completely I realized this truth. None but those who have visited this most wonderful valley can even imagine the feelings with which I looked upon the view that was there presented. The grandeur of the scene was but softened by the haze that hung over the valley—light as gossamer—and by the clouds which partially dimmed the higher cliffs and mountains. This obscurity of vision but increased the awe with which I beheld it, and as I looked, a peculiar exalted sensation seemed to fill my whole being, and I found my eyes in tears with emotion.

During many subsequent visits to this locality, this sensation was never again so fully aroused. It is probable that the shadows fast clothing all before me, and the vapory clouds at the head of the valley, leaving the view beyond still undefined, gave a weirdness to the scene, that made it so impressive; and the conviction that it was utterly indescribable added strength to the emotion. It is not possible for the same intensity of feeling to be aroused more than once by the same object, although I never looked upon these scenes except with wonder and admiration.

On our first visit, our imagination had been misled by the descriptive misrepresentations of savages, whose prime object was to keep us from their safe retreat, until we had expected to see some terrible abyss. The reality so little resembled the picture of imagination, that my astonishment was the more overpowering.

To obtain a more distinct and *quiet* view, I had left the trail and my horse and wallowed through the snow alone to a projecting granite rock. So interested was I in the scene before me, that I did not observe that my comrades had all moved on, and that I would soon be left indeed alone. My situation attracted the attention of Major Savage—who was riding in rear of column—who hailed me from the trail below with, "you had better wake up from that dream up there, or you may lose your hair; I have no faith in Ten-ie-ya's statement that there are no Indians about here. We had better be moving; some of the murdering devils may be lurking along this trail to pick off stragglers." I hurriedly joined the major on the descent, and as other views presented themselves, I said with some enthusiasm, "If my hair is now required, I can depart in peace, for I have here seen the power and glory of a Supreme being; the majesty of His handy-work is in that 'Testimony of the Rocks.' That mute appeal—pointing to El Capitan—illustrates it, with more convincing eloquence than can the most powerful arguments of surpliced priests." "Hold up, Doc! you are soaring too high for me; and perhaps for yourself. This is rough riding; we had better mind this

BRIDAL VEIL FALL.

devilish trail, or we shall go *soaring* over some of these slippery rocks.'' We, however, made the descent in safety. When we overtook the others we found blazing fires started and preparations commenced to provide supper for the hungry command; while the light-hearted ''boys'' were indulging their tired horses with the abundant grass found on the meadow near by, which was but lightly covered with snow.

MY devout astonishment at the supreme grandeur of the scenery by which I was surrounded continued to engross my mind. The warmth of the fires and preparations for supper, however, awakened in me other sensations, which rapidly dissipated my excitement. As we rode up, Major Savage remarked to Capt. Boling, ''We had better move on up and hunt out the 'Grizzlies' before we go into camp for the night. We shall yet have considerable time to look about this hole before dark.'' Captain Boling then reported that the young guide had halted here, and poured out a volley of Indian lingo which no one could understand, and had given a negative shake of his head when the course was pointed out, and signs were made for him to move on. The captain, not comprehending this performance, had followed the trail of the Indians to the bank of the stream near by, but had not ventured further, thinking it best to wait for Major Savage to come up. After a few inquiries the major said there was a ford below, where the Indians crossed the Merced; and that he would go with the guide and examine it. Major Savage and Captains Boling and Dill then started down to the crossing. They soon returned, and we were ordered to arrange our camp for the night. Captain Boling said the Merced was too high to ford. The river had swollen during the day from the melting of the snow, but would fall again by morning.

The guide had told the major there was no other way up the valley, as it was impossible to pass the rocks on the south side of the stream. From this, it was evident the major had never before seen the valley, and upon inquiry, said so. One of our best men, Tunnehill, who had been listening to what the captain was saying, very positively remarked: "I have long since learned to discredit everything told by an Indian. I never knew one to tell the truth. This imp of Satan has been lying to the major, and to me his object is very transparent. He knows a better ford than the one below us." A comrade laughingly observed: "Perhaps you can find it for the major, and help him give us an evening ride; I have had all the exercise I need today, and feel as hungry as a wolf." Without a reply, Tunnehill mounted his little black mule and left at a gallop. He returned in a short time, at the same rapid gate, but was in a sorry plight. The mule and rider had unexpectedly taken a plunge bath in the ice-cold waters of the Merced. As such mishaps excited but little sympathy, Tunnehill was greeted with, "Hello! what's the matter, comrade?" "Where do you get your washing done?" "Been trying to cool off that frisky animal, have you?" "Old Ten-ie-ya's cañon is not in as hot a place as we supposed, is it?" "How about the reliability of the Indian race?" To all these bantering jokes, though in an uncomfortable plight, Tunnehill, with great good nature, replied: "I am all right! I believe in orthodox immersion, but this kind of baptism has only *confirmed* me in previous convictions." The shivering mule was rubbed, blanketed, and provided for, before his master attended to his own comfort, and then we learned that, in his attempt to explore a way across the Merced, his mule was swept off its feet, and both were carried for some distance down the raging torrent.

After supper, guards stationed, and the camp fires plentifully provided for, we gathered around the burning logs of oak and pine, found near our camp. The hearty supper and cheerful blaze created a general good feeling. Social converse and anecdotes—mingled with jokes—were freely exchanged, as we enjoyed the solace of our pipes and warmed ourselves preparatory to seeking further refreshment in sleep. While thus engaged, I retained a full consciousness of our locality; for, being in close proximity to the huge cliff that had so attracted my attention, my mind was frequently drawn away from my comrades. After the jollity of the camp had somewhat subsided, the valley became the topic of conversation around our camp fire.

EL CAPITAN; 3,300 FEET HIGH.

None of us at that time surmised the extreme vastness of those cliffs; although before dark, we had seen El Capitan looking down upon our camp, while the "Bridal Veil" was being wafted in the breeze. Many of us *felt* the mysterious grandeur of the scenery, as defined by our limited opportunity to study it. I had—previous to my descent with the major—observed the towering height above us of the old "Rock Chief," and noticing the length of the steep descent into the valley, had at least some idea of its solemn immensity.

It may appear *sentimental,* but the coarse jokes of the careless, and the indifference of the practical, sensibly jarred my more devout feelings, while this subject was a matter of general conversation; as if a sacred subject had been ruthlessly profaned, or the visible power of Deity disregarded. After relating my observations from the "Old Bear Valley Trail," I suggested that this valley should have an appropriate name by which to designate it, and in a tone of pleasantry, said to Tunnehill, who was drying his wet clothing by our fire, "You are the first white man that ever received any form of baptism in this valley, and you should be considered the proper person to give a baptismal name to the valley itself." He replied, "If whisky can be provided for such a ceremony, I shall be happy to participate; but if it is to be another cold-water affair, I have no desire to take a hand. I have done enough in that line for tonight." Timely jokes and ready repartee for a time changed the subject, but in the lull of this exciting pastime, some one remarked, "I like Bunnell's suggestion of giving this valley a name, and tonight is a good time to do it." "All right—if you have got one, show your hand," was the response of another. Different names were proposed, but none were satisfactory to a majority of our circle. Some romantic and foreign names were offered, but I observed that a very large number were canonical and Scripture names. From this I inferred that I was not the only one in whom religious emotions or thoughts had been aroused by the mysterious power of the surrounding scenery.

As I did not take a fancy to any of the names proposed, I remarked that "an American name would be the most appropriate;" that "I could not see any necessity for going to a foreign country for a name for American scenery—the grandest that had ever yet been looked upon. That it would be better to give it an Indian name than to import a strange and inexpressive one; that the name of the tribe who had occupied it would be more appropriate than any I had heard suggested." I then proposed "that we give the valley the name of Yo-sem-i-ty, as it was suggestive, euphonious, and certainly *American;* that by so doing, the name of the tribe of Indians which we met leaving their homes in this valley, perhaps never to return, would be perpetuated." I was here interrupted by Mr. Tunnehill, who impatiently exclaimed: "Devil take the Indians and their names! Why should we honor these vagabond murderers by perpetuating their name?" Another said: "I agree with Tunnehill; —— the Indians and their names. Mad Anthony's plan for me! Let's call this Paradise Valley." In reply, I said to the last speaker, "Still, for a young man with such *religious tendencies* they would be good objects on which to develop your Christianity." Unexpectedly, a hearty laugh was raised, which broke up further discussion, and before opportunity was given for any others to object to the name, John O'Neil, a rollicking Texan of Capt. Boling's company, vociferously announced to the whole camp the subject of our discussion, by saying, "Hear ye! Hear ye! Hear ye! A vote will now be taken to decide what name shall be given to this valley." The question of giving it the name of Yo-sem-i-ty was then explained; and upon a *viva voce* vote being taken, it was almost unanimously adopted. The name that was there and thus adopted by us, while seated around our camp fires, on the first visit of a white man to this remarkable locality, is the name by which it is now known to the world.

At the time I proposed this name, the signification of it (a grizzly bear) was not generally known to our battalion, although "the grizzlies" was frequently used to designate this tribe. Neither was it pronounced with uniformity. For a correct pronunciation, Major Savage was our best authority. He could speak the dialects of most of the mountain tribes in this part of California, but he confessed that he could not readily understand Ten-ie-ya, or the Indian guide, as they appeared to speak a Pai-ute jargon.

Major Savage checked the noisy demonstrations of our "Master of Ceremonies," but approvingly participated in our proceedings, and told us that the name was Yo-sem-i-ty, as pronounced by Ten-ie-ya, or O-soom-i-ty, as pronounced by some other bands; and that it signified a full-grown grizzly bear. He further stated that the name was given to old Ten-ie-ya's band, because of their lawless and predatory character.

As I had observed that the different tribes in Mariposa county differed somewhat in the pronunciation of this name, I asked an explanation of the fact. With a smile and a look, as if he suspected I was quizzing him, the major replied: "They only differ, as do the Swedes, Danes and Norwegians, or as in the different Shires of England; but you know well enough how similar in sound words may be of entirely different meaning, and how much depends on accent. I have found this to be the greatest difficulty a learner has to contend with."

After the name had been decided upon, the major narrated some of his experiences in the use of the general "sign language"—as a Rocky Mountain man—and his practice of it when he first came among the California Indians, until he had acquired their language. The major regarded the Kah-we-ah, as the parent language of the San Joaquin Valley Indians, while that in use by the other mountain tribes in their vicinity, were but so many dialects of Kah-we-ah, the Pai-ute and more northern tribes. When we sought our repose it was with feelings of quiet satisfaction that I wrapped myself in my blankets, and soundly slept.

I consider it proper to digress somewhat from a regular narrative of the incidents of our expedition, to consider some matters relative to the name "Yosemity." This was the form of orthography and pronunciation originally in use by our battalion. Lieutenant Moore, of the U. S. A. in his report of an expedition to the valley in 1852, substituted e as the terminal letter, in place of y, in use by us; no doubt thinking the use of e more scholarly, or perhaps supposing Yosemite to be of Spanish derivation. This orthography has been adopted, and is in general use, but the proper pronunciation, as a consequence, is not always attainable to the general reader.

Some time after the name had been adopted, I learned from Major Savage that Ten-ie-ya repudiated the name for the valley, but proudly acknowledged it as the designation of his band, claiming that "when he was a young chief, this name had been selected because they occupied the mountains and valleys which were the favorite resort of the Grizzly Bears, and because his people were expert in killing them. That his tribe had adopted the name because those who had bestowed it were afraid of 'the Grizzlies' and feared his band."

It was traditionary with the other Indians, that the band to which the name Yosemite had been given, had originally been formed and was then composed of outlaws or refugees from other tribes. That nearly all were descendants of the neighboring tribes on both sides of "Kay-o-pha," or "*Skye Mountains;*" the "High Sierras."

Ten-ie-ya was asked concerning this tradition, and responded rather loftily: "I am the descendant of an Ah-wah-ne-chee chief. His people lived in the mountains and valley where my people have lived. The valley was then called Ah-wah-nee. Ah-wah-ne-chee signifies the dwellers in Ahwahnee."

I afterwards learned the traditional history of Ten-ie-ya's ancestors. His statement was to the effect that the Ah-wah-ne-chees had many years ago been a large tribe, and lived in territory now claimed by him and his people. That by wars, and a fatal black-sickness (probably smallpox or measles), nearly all had been destroyed. The survivors of the band fled from the valley and joined other tribes. For years afterward, the country was uninhabited; but few of the extinct tribe ever visited it, and from a superstitious fear, it was avoided. Some of his ancestors had gone to the Mono tribe and been adopted by them. His father had taken a wife from that tribe. His mother was a Mono woman, and he had lived with her people while young. Eventually, Ten-ie-ya, with some of his father's tribe, had visited the valley, and claimed it as their birthright. He thus became the founder of the new tribe or band, which has since been called the "Yosemite."

It is very probable that the statement of Major Savage, as to the origin of the name as applicable to Ten-ie-ya's band, was traditional with his informants, but I give credit to Ten-ie-ya's own history of his tribe as most probable.

From my knowledge of Indian customs, I am aware that it is not uncommon for them to change the names of persons or localities after some remarkable event in the history of either. It would not, therefore, appear strange that Ten-ie-ya should have adopted another name for his band. I was unable to fix upon any definite date at which the Ah-wah-ne-chees became extinct as a tribe, but from the fact that some of the Yosemites claimed to be direct descendants, the time could not have been as long as would be inferred from their descriptions. When these facts were communicated to Captain Boling, and Ah-wah-ne was ascertained to be the *classical* name, the captain said that name was all right enough for history or poetry, but that we could not now change the name Yosemite, nor was it desirable to do so. I made every effort to ascertain the signification of Ah-wah-ne, but could never fully satisfy myself, as I received different interpretations at different times. In endeavoring to ascertain from Ten-ie-ya his explanation of the name, he, by the motion of his hands, indicated depth, while trying to illustrate the name, at the same time plucking grass which he held up before me. From these *"signs"* I inferred that it must mean the deep grassy valley. Still, it may not mean that.

THE FIRST DRAWING MADE IN YOSEMITE
By Thomas Ayres, 1855

EXPLORING THE VALLEY

THE date of our discovery and entrance into the Yosemite was about the 21st of March, 1851. We were afterward assured by Ten-ie-ya and others of his band, that this was the first visit ever made to this valley by white men. Ten-ie-ya said that a small party of white men once crossed the mountains on the North side, but were so guided as not to see it; Appleton's and the People's Encyclopedias to the contrary notwithstanding.*

It was to prevent the recurrence of such an event that Ten-ie-ya had consented to go to the commissioner's camp and make peace, intending to return to his mountain home as soon as the excitement from the recent outbreak subsided. The entrance to the valley had ever been carefully guarded by the old chief, and the people of his band. As a part of its traditionary history, it was stated: ''That when Ten-ie-ya left the tribe of his mother and went to live in Ah-wah-ne, he was accompanied by a very old Ah-

---

*Captain Joe Walker, for whom ''Walker's Pass'' is named, told me that he once passed quite near the valley on one of his mountain trips; but that his Ute and Mono guides gave such a dismal account of the canons of both rivers, that he kept his course near to the divide until reaching Bull Creek, when he descended and went into camp, not seeing the valley proper.

wah-ne-chee, who had been the great 'medicine man' of his tribe.''

It was through the influence of this old friend of his father that Ten-ie-ya was induced to leave the Mono tribe, and with a few of the descendants from the Ah-wah-ne-chees, who had been living with the Monos and Pai-utes, to establish himself in the valley of his ancestors as their chief. He was joined by the descendants from the Ah-wah-ne-chees, and by others who had fled from their own tribes to avoid summary Indian justice. The old ''medicine man'' was the counselor of the young chief. Not long before the death of this patriarch, as if endowed with prophetic wisdom, he assured Ten-ie-ya that while he retained possession of Ah-wah-ne his band would increase in numbers and become powerful. That if he befriended those who sought his protection, no other tribe would come to the valley to make war upon him, or attempt to drive him from it, and if he obeyed his counsels he would put a spell upon it that would hold it sacred for him and his people alone; none other would ever dare to make it their home. He then cautioned the young chief against the horsemen of the lowlands (the Spanish residents), and declared that, should they enter Ah-wah-ne, his tribe would soon be scattered and destroyed, or his people be taken captive, and he himself be the last chief in Ah-wah-ne.

For this reason, Ten-ie-ya declared, had he so rigidly guarded his valley home, and all who sought his protection. No one ventured to enter it, except by his permission; all feared the ''witches'' there, and his displeasure. He had ''made war upon the white gold diggers to drive them from the mountains, and prevent their entrance into Ah-wah-ne.''

The Yo-sem-i-tes had been the most warlike of the mountain tribes in this part of California; and the Ah-wah-ne-

chee and Mono members of it, were of finer build and
lighter color than those commonly called "California Digger Indians." Even the "Diggers" of the band, from
association and the better food and air afforded in the
mountains, had become superior to their inheritance, and
as a tribe, the Yosemites were feared by other Indians.

The superstitious fear of annihilation had, however, so
depressed the warlike ardor of Ten-ie-ya, who had now
become an old man, that he had decided to make efforts to
conciliate the Americans, rather than further resist their
occupancy of the mountains; as thereby, he hoped to save
his valley from intrusion. In spite of Ten-ie-ya's cunning,
the prophecies of the "old medicine" man have been
mostly fulfilled. White horsemen have entered Ah-wah-ne;
the tribe has been scattered and destroyed. Ten-ie-ya was
the last chief of his people. He was killed by the chief of
the Monos, not because of the prophecy; nor yet because of
our entrance into his territory, but in retribution for a
crime against the Mono's hospitality. But I must not,
Indian like, tell the latter part of my story first.

After an early breakfast on the morning following our
entrance into the Yosemite, we equipped ourselves for
duty; and as the word was passed to "fall in," we mounted
and filed down the trail to the lower ford, ready to com-
mence our explorations.

The water in the Merced had fallen some during the
night, but the stream was still in appearance a raging torrent. As we were about to cross, our guide with earnest
gesticulations asserted that the water was too deep to cross;
that if we attempted it, we would be swept down into the
cañon; that later we could cross without difficulty. These
assertions angered the major, and he told the guide that he
lied; for he knew that later in the day the snow would melt.
Turning to Captain Boling he said: "I am now positive

that the Indians are in the vicinity, and for that reason the guide would deceive us." Telling the young Indian to remain near his person, he gave the order to cross at once.

The ford was found to be rocky; but we passed over it without serious difficulty, although several repeated their morning ablutions while stumbling over the boulders.

The open ground on the north side was found free from snow. The trail led toward "El Capitan," which had from the first been the particular object of my admiration.

At this time no distinctive names were known by which to designate the cliffs, waterfalls, or any of the especial objects of interest, and the imaginations of some ran wild in search of *appropriate* ones. None had any but a limited idea of the height of this cliff, and but few appeared conscious of the vastness of the granite wall before us; although an occasional ejaculation betrayed the feelings which the imperfect comprehension of the grand and wonderful excited. A few of us remarked upon the great length of time required to pass it and by so doing, probably arrived at more or less correct conclusions regarding its size.

Soon after we crossed the ford, smoke was seen to issue from a cluster of manzanita shrubs that commanded a view of the trail. On examination, the smoking brands indicated that it had been a picket fire, and we now felt assured that our presence was known and our movements watched by the vigilant Indians we were hoping to find. Moving rapidly on, we discovered near the base of El Capitan, quite a large collection of Indian huts, situated near Pigeon creek. On making a hasty examination of the village and vicinity, no Indians could be found, but from the generally undisturbed condition of things usually found in an Indian camp, it was evident that the occupants had but recently left; appearances indicated that some of the wigwams or huts had been occupied during the night. Not far from the camp, upon posts, rocks, and in trees, was a large *caché* of acorns and other provisions.

As the trail showed that it had been used by Indians going up, but a short halt was made. As we moved on, a smoke was again seen in the distance, and some of the more eager ones dashed ahead of the column, but as we reached the ford to which we were led by the main trail leading to the right, our dashing cavaliers rejoined us and again took their places. These men reported that "fallen rocks" had prevented their passage up on the north side, and that our only course was to cross at the ford and follow the trail, as the low lands appeared too wet for rapid riding. Recrossing the Merced to the south side, we found trails leading both up and down the river. A detachment was sent down to reconnoitre the open land below, while the main column

CACHES, OR INDIAN ACORN STOREHOUSES.

NORTH DOME AND ROYAL ARCHES.

pursued its course. The smoke we had seen was soon discovered to be rising from another encampment nearly south
of the "Royal Arches;" and at the forks of the Ten-ie-ya
branch of the Merced, near the southwest base of the "Half
Dome," still another group of huts was brought to view.

These discoveries necessitated the recrossing of the river,
which had now again become quite swollen; but by this
time our horses and ourselves had become used to the icy
waters, and when at times our animals lost their footing at
the fords, they were not at all alarmed, but vigorously
swam to the shore.

Abundant evidences were again found to indicate that
the huts here had but just been deserted; that they had
been occupied that morning. Although a rigid search was
made, no Indians were found. Scouting parties in charge
of Lieutenants Gilbert and Chandler, were sent out to
examine each branch of the valley, but this was soon found
to be an impossible task to accomplish in one day. While
exploring among the rocks that had fallen from the "Royal

Arches" at the southwesterly base of the North Dome, my attention was attracted to a huge rock stilted upon some smaller ones. Cautiously glancing underneath, I was for a moment startled by a living object. Involuntarily my rifle was brought to bear on it, when I discovered the object to be a female; an extremely old squaw, but with a countenance that could only be likened to a vivified Egyptian mummy. This creature exhibited no expression of alarm, and was apparently indifferent to hope or fear, love or hate. I hailed one of my comrades on his way to camp, to report to Major Savage that I had discovered a peculiar living ethnological curiosity, and to bring something for it to eat. She was seated on the ground, hovering over the remnants of an almost exhausted fire. I replenished her supply of fuel, and waited for the major. She neither spoke or exhibited any curiosity as to my presence.

Major Savage soon came, but could elicit nothing of importance from her. When asked where her companions were, she understood the dialect used, for she very curtly replied "You can hunt for them if you want to see them!" When asked why she was left alone, she replied "I am too old to climb the rocks!" The major—forgetting the gallantry due her sex—inquired "How old are you?" With an ineffably scornful grunt, and a coquettish leer at the major, she maintained an indignant silence. This attempt at a smile left the major in doubt as to her age. Subsequently, when Ten-ie-ya was interrogated as to the age of this old squaw, he replied that "No one knows her age. That when he was a boy it was a favorite *tradition* of the *old* members of his band, that when she was a child, the peaks of the Sierras were but little hills." This free interpretation was given by the major, while seated around the camp fire at night. If not *reliable,* it was excessively amusing to the "boys," and added to the major's popularity. On

CATHEDRAL ROCKS.

a subsequent visit to the valley an attempt was made to send the old creature to the commissioners' camp; she was placed on a mule and started. As she could not bear the fatigue, she was left with another squaw. We learned that she soon after departed "to *the happy land in the West*."

The detachment sent down the trail reported the discovery of a small rancheria, a short distance above the "Cathedral Rocks," but the huts were unoccupied. They also reported the continuance of the trail down the left bank. The other detachments found huts in groups, but no Indians. At all of these localities the stores of food were abundant.

Their *cachés* were principally of acorns, although many contained bay (California laurel), Piñon pine (Digger pine), and chinquepin nuts, grass seeds, wild rye or oats (scorched), dried worms, scorched grasshoppers, and what proved to be the dried larvæ of insects, which I was afterwards told were gathered from the waters of the lakes in and east of the Sierra Nevada. It was by this time quite clear that a large number of Ten-ie-ya's band was hidden in the cliffs or among the rocky gorges or cañons, not accessible to us from the knowledge we then had of their trails and passes. We had not the time, nor had we supplied ourselves sufficiently to hunt them out. It was therefore decided that the best policy was to destroy their huts and stores, with a view of starving them out, and of thus compelling them to come in and join with Ten-ie-ya and the people with him on the reservation. At this conclusion the destruction of their property was ordered, and at once commenced. While this work was in progress, I indulged my curiosity in examining the lodges in which had been left their home property, domestic, useful and ornamental. As compared with eastern tribes, their supplies of furniture of all kinds, excepting baskets, were meagre enough.

These baskets were quite numerous, and were of various patterns and for different uses. The large ones were made either of bark, roots of the Tamarach or Cedar, Willow or Tule. Those made for gathering and transporting food supplies were of large size and round form, with a sharp apex, into which, when inverted and placed upon the back, everything centers. This form of basket enables the carriers to keep their balance while passing over seemingly impassable rocks, and along the verge of dangerous precipices. Other baskets found served as water buckets. Others again of various sizes were used as cups and soup bowls; and still another kind, made of a tough, wiry grass, closely woven and cemented, was used for kettles for boiling food. The boiling was effected by hot stones being continually plunged into the liquid mass, until the desired result was obtained.

The water baskets were also made of "wire-grass;" being porous, evaporation is facilitated, and like the porous earthen water-jars of Mexico, and other hot countries, the water put into them is kept cool by evaporation. There were also found at some of the encampments, robes or blankets made from rabbit and squirrel skins, and from skins of water-fowl. There were also ornaments and musical instruments of a rude character. The instruments were drums and flageolets. The ornaments were of bone, bears' claws, birds' bills and feathers. The thread used by these Indians, I found was spun or twisted from the inner bark of a species of the asclepias or milk-weed, by ingeniously suspending a stone to the fibre, and whirling it with great rapidity. Sinews are chiefly used for sewing skins, for covering their bows and feathering their arrows. Their fish spears were but a single tine of bone, with a cord so attached near the centre, that when the spear, loosely placed in a socket in the pole, was pulled out by the struggles of the fish, the tine and cord would hold it as securely as though held by a barbed hook.

There were many things found that only an Indian could possibly use, and which it would be useless for me to attempt to describe; such, for instance, as stag-horn hammers, deer prong punches (for making arrow-heads), obsidian, pumice-stone and salt brought from the eastern slope of the Sierras and from the desert lakes. In the hurry of their departure they had left everything. The numerous bones of animals scattered about the camps indicated their love of horse-flesh as a diet.

Among these relics could be distinguished the bones of horses and mules, as well as other animals, eaten by these savages. Deers and bears were frequently driven into the valley during their seasons of migration, and were killed by expert hunters perched upon rocks and in trees that commanded their runways or trails; but their chief dependence for meat was upon horseflesh.

Among the relics of stolen property were many things recognized by our "boys," while applying the torch and giving all to the flames. A comrade discovered a bridle and part of a riata or rope which was stolen from him with a mule *while waiting for the commissioners to inquire into the cause of the war with the Indians!* No animals of any kind were kept by the Yosemites for any length of time except dogs, and they are quite often sacrificed to gratify their pride and appetite in a dog feast. Their highest estimate of animals is only as an article of food. Those stolen from the settlers were not kept for their usefulness, except as additional camp supplies. The acorns found were alone estimated at from four to six hundred bushels.

During our explorations we were on every side astonished at the colossal representations of cliffs, rocky cañons and waterfalls which constantly challenged our attention and admiration.

Occasionally some fragment of a garment was found, or other sign of Indians, but no trail could be discovered by *our* eyes. Tired and almost exhausted in the fruitless search for Indians, the footmen returned to the place at which they had left their horses in the cañons, and in very thankfulness caressed them with delight.

In subsequent visits, this region was thoroughly explored and names given to prominent objects and localities.

While searching for hidden stores, I took the opportunity to examine some of the numerous sweat-houses noticed on the bank of the Merced, below a large camp near the mouth of the Ten-ie-ya branch. It may not be out of place to here give a few words in description of these conveniences of a permanent Indian encampment, and the uses for which they are considered a necessity.

The remains of these structures are sometimes mistaken for Tumuli. They were constructed of poles, bark, grass and mud. The frame-work of poles is first covered with bark, reeds or grass, and then the mud—as tenacious as the soil will admit of—is spread thickly over it. The structure is in the form of a dome, resembling a huge round mound. After being dried by a slight fire, kindled inside, the mud is covered with earth of a sufficient depth to shed the rain from without, and prevent the escape of heat from within. A small opening for ingress and egress is left; this comprises the extent of the house when complete, and ready for use. These sweat-baths are used as a luxury, as a curative for disease, and as a convenience for cleansing the skin, when necessity demands it, although the Indian race is not noted for cleanliness.

As a luxury, no Russian or Turkish bath is more enjoyed by civilized people than are these baths by the Mountain

Indians. I have seen a half dozen or more enter one of these rudely constructed sweat-houses, through the small aperture left for the purpose. Hot stones are taken in, the aperture is closed until suffocation would seem impending, when they would crawl out reeking with perspiration, and with a shout, spring like acrobats into the cold waters of the stream. As a remedial agent for disease, the same course is pursued, though varied at times by the burning and inhalation of resinous boughs and herbs.

In the process for cleansing the skin from impurities, hot air alone is generally used. If an Indian had passed the usual period for mourning for a relative, and the adhesive pitch too tenaciously clung to his no longer sorrowful countenance, he would enter, and re-enter the heated house until the cleansing had become complete.

The mourning pitch is composed of the charred bones and ashes of their dead relative or friend. These remains of the funeral pyre, with the charcoal, are pulverized and mixed with the resin of the pine. This hideous mixture is usually retained upon the face of the mourner until it wears off. If it has been well compounded, it may last nearly a year; although the young—either from a superabundance of vitality, excessive reparative powers of the skin, or from powers of will—seldom mourn so long. When the bare surface exceeds that covered by the pitch, it is not a scandalous disrespect in the young to remove it entirely; but a mother will seldom remove pitch or garment until both are nearly worn out.

In their camps were found articles from the miners' camps, and from the unguarded "ranchman." There was no lack of evidence that the Indians who had deserted their villages or wigwams, were truly entitled to the *soubriquet* of "the Grizzlies," "the lawless."

Although we repeatedly discovered fresh trails leading from the different camps, all traces were soon lost among the rocks at the base of the cliffs. The débris or talus not only afforded places for temporary concealment, but provided facilities for escape without betraying the direction. If by chance a trail was followed for awhile, it would at last be traced to some apparently inaccessible ledge, or to the foot of some slippery depression in the walls, up which we did not venture to climb. While scouting up the Ten-ie-ya Cañon, above Mirror Lake, I struck the fresh trail of quite a large number of Indians. Leaving our horses, a few of us followed up the tracks until they were lost in the ascent up the cliff. By careful search they were again found and followed until finally they hopelessly disappeared.

Tiring of our unsuccessful search, the hunt was abandoned, although we were convinced that the Indians had in some way passed up the cliff.

During this time, and while descending to the valley, I partly realized the great height of the cliffs and high fall. I had observed the height we were compelled to climb before the Talus had been overcome, though from below this appeared insignificant, and after reaching the summit of our ascent, the cliffs still towered above us. It was by instituting these comparisons while ascending and descending that I was able to form a better judgment of altitude; for while entering the valley—although, as before stated, I had observed the towering height of El Capitan—my mind had been so preoccupied with the marvelous, that comparison had scarcely performed its proper function.

The level of the valley proper now appeared quite distant as we looked down upon it, and objects much less than full size. As night was fast approaching, and a storm threatened, we returned down the trail and took our course

MIRROR LAKE ; WATKINS' AND CLOUDS' REST.

for the rendezvous selected by Major Savage, in a grove of oaks near the mouth of "Indian Cañon."

While on our way down, looking across to and up the south or Glacier Cañon, I noticed its beautiful fall, and planned an *excursion* for the morrow. I almost forgot my fatigue, in admiration of the solemn grandeur within my view; the lofty walls, the towering domes and numerous water-falls; their misty spray blending with the clouds settling down from the higher mountains.

The duties of the day had been severe on men and horses, for beside fording the Merced several times, the numerous branches pouring over cliffs and down ravines from the melting snow rendered the overflow of the bottom lands so constant that we were often compelled to splash through the water courses that later would be dry. These torrents of cold water commanded more especial attention, and excited more *comment* than did the grandeur of the cliffs and water-falls. We were not a party of tourists, seeking recreation, nor philosophers investigating the operations of nature. Our business there was to find Indians who were endeavoring to escape from our *charitable* intentions toward them. But very few of the volunteers seemed to have any appreciation of the wonderful proportions of the enclosing granite rocks; their curiosity had been to see the stronghold of the enemy, and the *general* verdict was that it was gloomy enough.

VERNAL FALLS: 350 FEET HIGH.

NEVADA FALLS: 700 FEET HIGH.

Tired and wet, the independent scouts sought the camp
and reported their failures. Gilbert and Chandler came in
with their detachments just at dark, from their tiresome
explorations of the southern branches. Only a small squad
of their commands climbed above the Vernal and Nevada
falls; and seeing the clouds resting upon the mountains
above the Nevada Fall, they retraced their steps through
the showering mist of the Vernal, and joined their com-

rades, who had already started down its rocky gorge. These men found no Indians, but they were the first discoverers of the Vernal and Nevada Falls, and the Little Yosemite. They reported what they had seen to their assembled comrades at the evening camp-fires. Their names have now passed from my memory—not having had an intimate personal acquaintance with them—for according to my recollection they belonged to the company of Capt. Dill.

While on our way down to camp we met Major Savage with a detachment who had been burning a large *caché* located in the fork, and another small one below the mouth of the Ten-ie-ya branch. This had been held in reserve for possible use, but the major had now fired it, and the flames were leaping high. Observing his movements for a few moments we rode up and made report of our unsuccessful efforts. I briefly, but with some enthusiasm, described my view from the cliff up the North Cañon, the Mirror Lake view of the Half Dome, the fall of the South Cañon and the view of the distant South Dome. I volunteered a suggestion that some new tactics would have to be devised before we should be able to corral the "Grizzlies" or "smoke them out." The major looked up from the charred mass of burning acorns, and as he glanced down the smoky valley, said: "This affords us the best prospect of any yet discovered; just look!" "Splendid!" I promptly replied, Yo-sem-i-te must be beautifully grand a few weeks later when the foliage and flowers are at their prime, and the rush of water has somewhat subsided. Such cliffs and water-falls I never saw before, and I doubt if they exist in any other place."

I was surprised and somewhat irritated by the hearty laugh with which my reply was greeted. The major caught the expression of my eye and shrugged his shoulders as he hastily said "I suppose that is all right, Doctor, about the

water-falls, etc., for there are enough of them here for one
locality, as we have all discovered; but my remark was not
in reference to the scenery, but the *prospect* of the Indians
being starved out, and of their coming in to sue for peace.
We have all been more or less wet since we rolled up our
blankets this morning, and this fire is very enjoyable, but
the prospect that it offers to my mind of *smoking out* the
Indians is more agreeable to me than its warmth or all the
scenery in creation. I know, Doc, that there is a good deal
of iron in you, but there is also considerable sentiment, and
I am not in a very sentimental mood." I replied that I
did not think that any of us felt very much like making
love or writing poetry, but that Ten-ie-ya's remark to him
about the "Great Spirit" providing so bountifully for his
people had several times occurred to me since entering
here, and that no doubt to Ten-ie-ya, this was a veritable
Indian paradise. "Well," said the major, "as far as that
is concerned, although I have not carried a Bible with me
since I became a mountain man, I remember well enough
that Satan entered paradise and did all the mischief he
could, but I intend to be a bigger devil in this Indian paradise than old Satan ever was; and when I leave, I don't
intend to *crawl* out, either. Now, Doc, we will go to camp,
but let me say while upon the subject, that we are in no
condition to judge fairly of this valley. The annoyances
and disappointments of a fruitless search, together with
the certainty of a snowstorm approaching, makes all this
beautiful scenery appear to me gloomy enough. In a word,
it is what we supposed it to be before seeing it, a h— of a
place. The valley, no doubt, will always be a wonder for
its grouping of cliffs and water-falls, but hemmed in by
walls of rock, your vision turned in, as it were, upon yourself—a residence here would be anything but desirable for
me. Any one of the Rocky Mountain parks would be pref-

erable, while the ease with which buffalo, black-tail and big-horn could be provided in the "Rockies" would, in comparison, make your Indian paradise anything but desirable, even for these Indians."

The more practical tone and views of the major dampened the ardor of my fancy in investing the valley with all desirable qualities, but as we compared with each other the experiences of the day, it was very clear that the half had not yet been seen or told, and that repeated views would be required before any one person could say that he had seen the Yosemite. It will probably be as well for me to say here that though Major Savage commanded the first expedition to the valley, he never revisited it, and died without ever having seen the Vernal and Nevada Falls, or any of the views belonging to the region of the Yosemite, except those seen from the valley and from the old Indian trail on our first entrance.

We found our camp had been plentifully supplied with dry wood by the provident guard, urged, no doubt, by the threatening appearances of another snow-storm. Some rude shelters of poles and brush were thrown up around the fires, on which were placed the drying blankets, the whole serving as an improvement on our bivouac accommodations. The night was colder than the previous one, for the wind was coming down the cañons of the snowy Sierras. The fires were lavishly piled with the dry oak wood, which sent out a glowing warmth. The fatigue and exposure of the day were forgotten in the hilarity with which supper was devoured by the hungry scouts while steaming in their wet garments. After supper Major Savage announced that "from the very extensive draft on the commissary stores just made, it was necessary to return to the 'South Fork.' " He said that it would be advisable for us to return, as we were not in a condition to endure delay if the threatened storm should prove to be a severe one; and ordered both Captains Boling and Dill to have their companies ready for the march at daylight the next morning.

While enjoying the warmth of the fire preparatory to a night's rest, the incidents of our observations during the day were interchanged. The probable heights of the cliffs was discussed. One *official* estimated "El Capitan" at 400 feet! Capt. Boling at 800 feet; Major Savage was in no mood to venture an opinion. My estimate was a sheer perpendicularity of at least 1500 feet. Mr. C. H. Spencer, son of Prof. Thomas Spencer of Geneva, N. Y.—who had traveled quite extensively in Europe—and a French gentleman, Monsieur Bouglinval, a civil engineer, who had joined us for the sake of adventure, gave me their opinions that my estimate was none too high; that it was probable that I was far below a correct measurement, for when there was so much sameness of height the judgment could not very well be assisted by comparison, and hence instrumental measurements alone could be relied on. Time has demonstrated the correctness of their opinions. These gentlemen were men of education and practical experience in observing the heights of objects of which measurement had been made, and quietly reminded their auditors that it was difficult to measure such massive objects with the eye alone. That some author had said: "But few persons have a correct judgment of height that rises above sixty feet."

I became somewhat earnest and enthusiastic on the subject of the valley, and expressed myself in such a positive manner that the *"enfant terrible"* of the company derisively asked if I was given to exaggeration before I became an "Indian fighter." From my ardor in description, and admiration of the scenery, I found myself nicknamed "Yosemity" by some of the battalion. It was customary among the mountain men and miners to prefix distinctive names.

From this hint I became less *expressive*, when conversing on matters relating to the valley. My self-respect caused me to talk less among my comrades generally, but with intimate friends the subject was always an open one, and my estimates of heights were never reduced.

Major Savage took no part in this camp discussion, but on our expressing a design to revisit the valley at some future time, he assured us that there was a probability of our being fully gratified, for if the renegades did not voluntarily come in, another visit would soon have to be made by the battalion, when we could have opportunity to measure the rocks if we then desired; that we should first escort our "captives" to the commissioners' camp on the Fresno; that by the time we returned to the valley the trails would be clear of snow, and we would be able to explore to our satisfaction. Casting a quizzing glance at me, he said: "The rocks will probably keep, but you will not find all of these immense *water-powers*."

Notwithstanding a little warmth of discussion, we cheerfully wrapped ourselves in our blankets and slept, until awakened by the guard; for there had been no disturbance during the night. The snow had fallen only to about the depth of an inch in the valley, but the storm still continued.

By early dawn "all ready" was announced, and we started back without having seen any of the Indian race except our useless guide and the old squaw. Major Savage rode at the head of the column, retracing our trail, rather than attempt to follow down the south side. The water was relatively low in the early morning, and the fords were passed without difficulty. While passing El Capitan I felt like saluting, as I would some dignified acquaintance.

The *cachés* below were yet smouldering, but the lodges had disappeared.

At our entrance we had closely followed the Indian trail over rocks that could not be re-ascended with animals. To return, we were compelled to remove a few obstructions of poles, brush and loose rocks, placed by the Indians to prevent the escape of the animals stolen and driven down. Entire herds had been sometimes taken from the ranches or their ranges.

After leaving the valley, but little difficulty was encountered. The snow had drifted into the hollows, but had not to any extent obscured the trail, which we now found quite hard. We reached the camp earlier in the day than we had reason to expect. During these three days of absence from headquarters, we had discovered, named and partially explored one of the most remarkable of the geographical wonders of the world.

"THE FORD-ENTRANCE TO YOSEMITE VALLEY, CALIFORNIA",
BY THOMAS AYRES, 1855

CAPTAIN JOHN BOLING

REMOVAL TO FRESNO; ESCAPE EN ROUTE

ON our arrival at the rendezvous on the South Fork the officer in charge reported: "We are about out of grub." This was a satisfactory cause for a hurried movement; for a short allowance had more terrors for men with our appetites than severe duties; and most of us had already learned that, even with prejudice laid aside, our stomachs would refuse the hospitalities of the Indians, if it were possible for them to share with us from their own scanty stores. The major's experience prompted him at once to give the order to break camp and move on for the camp on the Fresno.

Our mounted force chafed at the slowness of our march, for the Indians could not be hurried. Although their cookery was of the most primitive character, we were very much delayed by the time consumed in preparing their food.

While traveling we were compelled to accommodate our movements to the capacities or inclinations of the women and children. Capt. Dill, therefore, with his company was sent on ahead from the crossing of the South Fork, they leaving with us what food they could spare. When Dill reached the waters of the Fresno about one hundred "captives" joined him. These Indians voluntarily surrendered to Captain Dill's company, which at once hurried them on, and they reached the commissioners at the Fresno.

Captain Boling's company and Major Savage remained with the "Grand Caravan," keeping out scouts and hunters to secure such game as might be found to supply ourselves with food. We had no anxiety for the safety or security of our "captives;" our own subsistence was the important consideration; for the first night out from Bishop's camp left us but scanty stores for breakfast. Our halting places were selected from the old Indian camping grounds, which were supplied with hoyas (holes or mortars). These permanent mortars were in the bed-rock, or in large detached rocks that had fallen from the cliffs or mountains. These "hoyas" had been formed and used by past generations. They were frequent on our route, many of them had long been abandoned; as there was no indications of recent uses having been made of them. From their numbers it was believed that the Indians had once been much more numerous than at that date.

By means of the stone pestles with which they were provided, the squaws used these primitive mills to reduce their acorns and grass seeds to flour or meal. While the grists were being ground, others built the fires on which stones were heated.

When red hot, these stones were plunged into baskets nearly filled with water; this is continued until the water boils. The stones are then removed and the acorn meal, or a cold mixture of it, is stirred in until thin gruel is made; the hot stones are again plunged into the liquid mass and again removed. When sufficiently cooked, this "Atola" or porridge, was poured into plates or moulds of sand, prepared for that purpose. During the process of cooling, the

excess of water leaches off through the sand, leaving the woody fibre tannin and unappropriated coarse meal in distinctive strata; the edible portion being so defined as to be easily separated from the refuse and sand. This preparation was highly prized by them, and contrary to preconceived ideas and information, all of the Indians I asked assured me that the *bitter* acorns were the best when cooked. This compound of acorn meal resembles corn starch blanc mange in color, but is more dense in consistency. Although it was free from grit, and comparatively clean, none of us were able to eat it, and we were quite hungry. From this, I was led to conclude that to relish this Indian staple, the taste must be acquired while very young.

Old Ten-ie-ya's four wives, and other squaws, were disposed to be quite hospitable when they learned that our supply of provisions was exhausted. None of the command, however, ventured to sample their acorn-jellies, grass-seed mush, roasted grasshoppers, and their other delicacies; nothing was accepted but the Piñon pine nuts, which were generally devoured with a relish and a regret for the scarcity.

Certain species of worms, the larvæ of ants and some other insects, common mushrooms and truffles, or wood-mushrooms, are prized by the Indian epicure, as are eels, shrimps, oysters, frogs, turtles, snails, etc., by his white civilized brother. Are we really but creatures of education?

The *baskets* used by the Indians for boiling their food and other purposes, as has been before stated, are made of a tough mountain bunch-grass, nearly as hard and as strong as wire, and almost as durable. So closely woven are they that but little if any water can escape from them. They are made wholly impervious with a resinous compound resembling the vulcanized rubber used by dentists. This composition does not appear to be in the least affected by hot water. The same substance, in appearance at least, is used by Mountain Indians in attaching sinews to bows, and feathers and barbs to arrows.

I endeavored to ascertain what the composition was, but could only learn that the resin was procured from small trees or shrubs, and that some substance (probably mineral) was mixed with it, the latter to resist the action of heat and moisture. I made a shrewd guess that pulverized lava and sulphur (abundant east of the High Sierras) was used, but for some cause I was left in ignorance. The Indians, like all ignorant persons, ascribe remarkable virtues to very simple acts and to inert remedies. Upon one occasion a doctor was extolling the virtues of a certain root, ascribing to it almost miraculous powers; I tried in vain to induce him to tell me the name of the root. He stated that the secret was an heirloom, and if told, the curative power of the plant would disappear; but he kindly gave me some as a preventive of some imaginary ill, when lo! I discovered the famous remedy to be the cowslip.

After a delayed and hungry march of several days, we halted near sundown within a few miles of the commissioners' headquarters, and went into camp for the night. The Indians came straggling in at will from their hunts on the way, their trophies of skill with their bows being the big California squirrels, rabbits or hares and quail. Our more expert white hunters had occasionally brought in venison for our use. We had ceased to keep a very effective guard over our "captives;" none seemed necessary, as all appeared contented and satisfied, almost joyous, as we neared their destination on the Fresno.

The truth is, we regarded hostilities, so far as these Indians were concerned, as ended. We had voted the peace policy a veritable success. We had discussed the matter in camp, and contrasted the lack of spirit exhibited by these people with what we knew of the warlike character of the Indians of Texas and of the northwestern plains. In these comparisons, respect for our captives was lost in contempt. "The noble red man" was not here represented. The only ones of the Pacific Slope, excepting the Navahoes, Pimas and Maricopahs, that bear any comparison with the Eastern tribes for intelligence and bravery, are the You-mahs of the Colorado river, the Modocs, and some of the Rogue and Columbia river tribes, but none of these really equal the Sioux and some other Eastern tribes.

Hardly any attention had been paid to the captives during the preceding night, except from the guard about our own camp; from a supposition that our services could well be spared. Application was therefore made by a few of us for permission to accompany the major, who had determined to go on to the Fresno headquarters. When consent was given, the wish was so generally expressed that Captain Boling with nine men to act as camp guard, volunteered to remain, if Major Savage would allow the hungry "boys" to ride with him. The major finally assented to the proposition, saying: "I do not suppose the Indians can be driven off, or be induced to leave until they have had the feast I promised them; besides, they will want to see some of the commissioners' finery. I have been delighting their imaginations with descriptions of the presents in store for them."

When the order was passed for the hungry squad to fall in, we mounted with grateful feelings towards Captain Boling, and the "boys" declared that the major was a trump, for his consideration of our need. With the prospect of a good "square" meal, and the hope of a genial "smile" from our popular commissary, the time soon passed, and the distance seemed shortened, for we entered the Fresno camp before our anticipations were cloyed.

Headquarters was well supplied with all needful comforts, and was not totally deficient in luxuries. Our quartermaster and commissary was active in his duties, and as some good women say of their husbands, "He was a good provider." We had no reason to complain of our reception; our urgent requirements were cheerfully met. The fullness of our entertainment did not prevent a good night's rest, nor interfere with the comfortable breakfast which we enjoyed. While taking coffee, the self-denial of Captain Boling and his volunteer guard was not forgotten. Arrangements were made to furnish the best edible and potable stores that could be secured from our conscientious and prudent commissary. We were determined to give them a glorious reception; but—the captain did not bring in his captives! Major Savage sent out a small detachment to ascertain the cause of the delay. This party filled their haversacks with comforts for the "Indian guard." After some hours of delay, the major became anxious to hear from Captain Boling, and began to be suspicious that something more serious than the loss of his animals was the cause of not sending in a messenger, and he ordered out another detachment large enough to meet any supposed emergency. Not far from camp they met the captain and his nine men (the *"Indian guard"*) and *one* Indian, with the relief party first sent out. Our jovial captain rode into "headquarters" looking more crest-fallen than he had ever been seen before. When asked by the major where he had left the Indians, he blushed like a coy maiden and said: "They have all gone to the mountains but the one I have with me."

After Captain Boling had made his report to the major, and made all explanations to the commissioners, and when he had refreshed himself with an extra ration or two of the potable liquid that by special stipulation had been reserved for the "Indian guard," something of his old humor returned to him, and he gave us the details of his annoyances by the breach of trust on the part of "our prisoners."

The captain said: "Soon after you left us last night, one of my men, who was out hunting when we camped, came in with a deer he had killed just at the dusk of the evening. From this we made a hearty supper, and allowed the youth who had helped to bring in the deer to share in the meat. The Indian cooked the part given to him at our fire, and ate with the avidity of a famished wolf. This excited comment, and anecdotes followed of the enormous appetites displayed by some of them. The question was then raised, 'how much can this Indian eat at one meal?' I suggested that a fair trial could not be had with only one deer. Our hunter said he would give him a preliminary trial, and when deer were plenty we could then test his full capacity, if he should prove a safe one to bet on. He then cut such pieces as we thought would suffice for our breakfast, and, with my approval, gave the remainder to his boy, who was anxiously watching his movements. I consented to this arrangement, not as a test of his capacity, for I had often seen a hungry Indian eat, but as a reward for his services in bringing in the deer on his shoulders. He readily re-commenced his supper, and continued to feast until every bone was cracked and picked. When the last morsel of the venison had disappeared he commenced a doleful sing-song, 'Way-ah-we-ha-ha, Wah-ah-we-ha-ha' to some unknown deity, or, if I was to judge from my ear of the music, it must have been his prayer to the devil, for I have heard that it is a part of their worship. His song was soon echoed from the camp where all seemed contentment. After *consoling* himself in this manner for some time he fell asleep at our fire.

"The performance being over, I told my men to take

their sleep and I would watch, as I was not sleepy; if I wanted them I would call them. I then thought, as Major Savage had declared, the Indians could scarcely be driven off, until they had had their feast and the presents they expected to have given them. I sat by the fire for a long time cogitating on past events and future prospects, when thinking it useless to require the men to stand guard, I told them to sleep. Moving about and seeing nothing but the usual appearance, I decided it to be unnecessary to exercise any further vigilance, and told one of the men, who was partially aroused by my movements, and who offered to get up and stand guard, that he had better lie still and sleep. Toward morning I took another round, and finding the Indian camp wrapped in apparently profound slumber, I concluded to take a little sleep myself, until daylight. This now seems unaccountable to me, for I am extremely cautious in my habits. Such a breach of military discipline would have subjected one of my men to a court-martial. I confess myself guilty of neglect of duty; I should have taken nothing for granted.

"No one can imagine my surprise and mortification when I was called and told that the Indian camp was entirely deserted, and that none were to be seen except the one asleep by our camp-fire. My indifference to placing a guard over the Indian camp will probably always be a mystery to me, but it most likely saved our lives, for if we had attempted to restrain them, and you know us well enough to believe we would not have let them off without a fight: they would probably have pretty well used us up. As it was, we did not give them up without an effort. We saddled our horses and started in chase, thinking that as while with us, their women and children would retard their progress, and that we would soon overtake them. We took the young brave with us, who had slept by our fire. He knew nothing of the departure of his people, and was very much alarmed, as he expected we would at once kill him. I tried to make him useful in following their trail; he by signs gave me to understand he did not know where they had gone, and seemed unwilling to take the trail when I pointed it out to him. He evidently meant to escape the first opportunity. I kept him near me and treated him kindly, but gave him to understand I should shoot him if he tried to leave me.

"We pursued until the trail showed that they had scattered in every direction in the brushy ravines and on the rocky side of a mountain covered with undergrowth, where we could not follow them with our animals. Chagrined and disgusted with myself for my negligence, and my inability to recover any part of my charge, and considering farther pursuit useless, we turned about and took the trail to headquarters with our one captive."

Major Savage took the youngster under his charge, and flattered him by his conversations and kindly treatment. The commissioners lionized him somewhat; he was gaily clothed and ornamented, loaded with presents for his own family relations, and was given his liberty and permitted to leave camp at his leisure, and thus departed the last of the "grand caravan" of some three hundred and fifty "captives," men, women and children, which we had collected and escorted from the mountains.

The sight of the one hundred brought to them by Captain Dill, and his report that we were coming with about three hundred and fifty more, aroused sanguine hopes in the commission that the war was over, and that their plans had been successful. "Now that the *prisoners* have fled," we asked, "What will be done?"

To a military man, this lack of discipline and precaution —through which the Indians escaped—will seem unpardonable; and an officer who, like our captain, should leave his camp unguarded, under any circumstances, would be deemed disgracefully incompetent. In palliation of these facts, it may not occur to the rigid disciplinarian that Captain John Boling and the men under him—or the most of them, had not had the advantages of army drill and discipline. The courage of these mountain men in times of danger was undoubted; their caution was more apt to be displayed in times of danger to others than when they themselves were imperiled.

In this case Captain Boling was not apprehensive of danger to those under his charge. His excessive good nature and good will toward his men prompted him to allow, even to command them, to take the sleep and rest that an irregular diet, and the labor of hunting while on the march, had seemed to require. No one had a keener sense of his error than himself. The whole command sympathized with him—notwithstanding the ludicrous aspect of the affair—their finer feelings were aroused by his extreme regrets. They determined that if opportunities offered, he should have their united aid to wipe out this stigma. Major Savage was deceived by the child-like simplicity with which the Indians had been talking to him of the feast expected, and of the presents they would soon receive from the commissioners. He did not suppose it possible that they would make an attempt to escape, or such a number would not have been left with so small a guard. We had men with us who knew what discipline was, who had been trained to obey orders without hesitation. Men who had fought under Col. Jack Hays, Majors Ben McCullough and Mike Chevallia, both in Indian and Mexican warfare, and they considered themselves well posted. Even these men were mistaken in their opinions. The sudden disappearance of the Indians was as much a surprise to them as to our officers.

With a view to solving this mystery Vow-ches-ter was sent for from his camp near by, where all the treaty tribes were congregated, and when questioned the chief said that during the night Chow-chilla runners had been in the camp, and to him in person with their mouths filled with lies; they had probably gone to the camp of those who were coming in, and they were induced to leave. Evidently he felt assured of the fact; but until questioned, his caution, Indian-like, kept him silent. Vow-ches-ter's sincerity and desire for peace was no longer doubted. Those who were suspicious of his friendship before were silenced, if not convinced, when he volunteered to go out and bring in such of the fugitives as he could convince of the good will of the commissioners. The young Indian had not yet left the camp, but was found relating his adventures and good fortune, and was directed to accompany Vow-ches-ter on his mission of good will. The chief was instructed to give positive assurances of protection against hostilities, if any were threatened by the Chow-chillas. He was also instructed to dispatch runners to aid his efforts, and was told to notify all that the commissioners would not remain to be trifled with; if they wished peace they must come in at once. That if the commissioners should go away, which they soon would do on their way south, no further efforts for peace would be made. That the mountain men and soldiers of the whites were angry, and would no longer take their word for peace, but would punish them and destroy their supplies. After a few days Vow-ches-ter came back with about one hundred of the runaways; these were followed by others, until ultimately, nearly all came back except Ten-ie-ya and his people. All then in camp expressed a readiness to meet for a grand council and treaty.

The reasons given by those who returned for their flight,

were that just before daylight on the morning of their departure Chow-chilla runners (as had been surmised by Vow-ches-ter) came to their camp with the report that they were being taken to the plains, where they would all be killed in order to evade the promises to pay for their lands, and for revenge.

In reply to the statements that they had been treated by the whites as friends, the Chow-chillas answered sneeringly that the whites were not fools to forgive them for killing their friends and relatives, and taking their property, and said their scouts had seen a large mounted force that was gathering in the foothills and on the plains, who would ride over them if they ventured into the open ground of the reservation, or encampment at the plains. This caused great alarm. They expected destruction from the whites, and in the excitement caused by the Chow-chillas, threatened to kill Captain Boling and his men, and for that purpose reconnoitered the captain's camp. The Chow-chillas dissuaded them from the attempt, saying: "The white men always sleep on their guns, and they will alarm the white soldiers below by their firing, and bring upon you a mounted force before you could reach a place of safety."

The young fellow that was asleep in Boling's camp was not missed until on the march; his appearance among them gaily clothed, after being kindly treated, very much aided Vow-ches-ter in his statement of the object of the council and treaty to be held. The runaways told the commissioners that they felt very foolish, and were ashamed that they had been so readily deceived; they also expressed a wish that we would punish the Chow-chillas, for they had caused all the trouble. The reception they received soon satisfied them that they had nothing to fear. They were given food and clothing, and their good fortune was made known to other bands, and soon all of the tribes in the vicinity made treaties or sent messengers to express their willingness to do so, excepting the Chow-chillas and Yosemites. Even Ten-ie-ya was reported to have ventured into the Indian quarter, but taking a look at the gaudy colored handkerchiefs and shirts offered him in lieu of his ancient and well-worn guernsey that he habitually wore, he scoffingly refused the offers. Turning towards his valley home, he sorrowfully departed; his feelings apparently irritated by the evidences of vanity he saw in the gaudy apparel and weak contentment of those he was leaving behind him. Major Savage, who it was supposed would be the Indian agent at the end of the war, was absent at the time of Ten-ie-ya's visit, but "the farmer" showed the old chief all proper respect, and had endeavored to induce him to await the major's return, but failed.

"FALLS OF AWANE", NEVADA FALLS BY THOMAS AYRES, 1856

STARVATION WARFARE: BACK TO THE YOSEMITE

MAJOR SAVAGE now advised a vigorous campaign against the Chow-chillas. The stampeding of our captives was one of the incentives for this movement; or at least, it was for this reason that Captain Boling and his company most zealously advocated prompt action. The commissioners approved of the plan, and decided that as the meddlesome interference of these Indians prevented other bands from coming in, it was necessary, if a peace policy was to be maintained with other tribes, that this one be made to feel the power they were opposing. Accordingly a force composed of B. and C. companies, Boling's and Dill's, numbering about one hundred men, under command of Major Savage, started for the San Joaquin river. The route selected was by way of "Coarse Gold Gulch," to the headwaters of the Fresno, and thence to the North Fork of the San Joaquin.

The object of taking this circuitous route was to sweep the territory of any scattered bands that might infest it.

As soon as Captain Boling was satisfied that we had accomplished, in this locality, all that could be expected of his command, we started for headquarters.

A FEW days after our return from the campaign against the Chow-chillas, a small delegation from a Kah-we-ah band on King's River was sent in by Captain Kuykendall, whose energy had subdued nearly all of the Indians in his department. The chief of this band informed Major Savage that Tom-kit and Frederico, successors in authority to José Rey, had visited his camp, and had reported that they were very hungry. They came, they said, to hold a council. The chief told the major that he had advised them to come in with him and make a treaty, but they refused. They said the white man's "medicine" was too powerful for them; but if their great chief had not died, he would have driven the white men from the mountains, for he was "a heap wise." The white soldiers had killed their great chief; they had killed many of their best warriors; they had burned up their huts and villages and destroyed their supplies, and had tried to drive their people from their territory, and they would kill their women and children if they did not hide them where they could not be found; and much more in a similar vein.

A small supply of acorns had been given these fugitives, and when the chief left, they had promised to return and hear what the commissioners had said. Major Savage reported this, and with the commissioners' approval, decided to return with the Kah-we-ah chief and meet in counsel with the Chow-chillas. He took with him sufficient "beef" on foot to give the Indians a grand feast, which lasted several days; during which time arrangements were completed for treaties with all of the remaining bands of the Kah-we-ah tribe, and with the Chow-chillas.

The Chow-chillas now being disposed of, and a treaty signed by the other tribes, it was decided by the commissioners that our next expedition should be against the Yo-sem-i-tes. This had been recommended by Major Savage as the only practical method of effecting any terms with their old chief. Every inducement had been offered them that had been successful with the others; but had been treated with contempt. The liberal supplies of beef they refused, saying they preferred horse-flesh. The half-civilized garbs and gaudy presents tendered at the agency were scorned by Ten-ie-ya as being no recompense for relinquishing the freedom of his mountain home. Major Savage announced that the expedition would start as soon as the floods had somewhat subsided, so that the streams could be crossed. As for ourselves, we had learned to take advantage of any narrow place in a stream, and by means of ropes stretched for feet and hands, we crossed without difficulty streams that we could not ford with horses. As this delay would allow an opportunity for some of the battalion to see to such private business as required their attention, short furloughs were granted to those most anxious to improve this occasion.

As the furloughs granted to the members of B and C companies expired, all promptly reported for duty, and preparations were completed for another campaign against the Yosemites.

As it was the design of Major Savage to make a thorough search in the territory surrounding the Yosemite, if we failed in surprising the inhabitants in their valley, a few scouts and guides were provided for the expedition to aid in our search among the "High Sierras," so distinctively named by Prof. Whitney. Among our ample supplies ropes were furnished, by order of Major Savage, suitable for floats, and for establishing bridges where needed. These bridges were suggested by myself, and were useful as a support while passing through swift water, or for crossing narrow but rushing torrents. This was accomplished expeditiously by simply stretching *"taut"* two ropes, one above the other, the upper rope, grasped by the hands, serving to secure the safe passage of the stream. Where trees were not found in suitable position to make the suspension, poles were lashed together so as to form *shears*, which served for trestles. I also suggested that snowshoes could probably be used with advantage on our mountain excursions. The use of these I found entirely unknown, except to Major Savage and a few other eastern men. My experience favored their use, as I had often found it easier to travel *over* deep snow than to wallow through it. My suggestion caused a *"heap"* of merriment, and my friend Chandler laughed until he became *"powerful weak,"* and finally I was assailed by so many shafts of witty raillery from my southern comrades, that I was willing to retreat, and cry out, "hold, enough!"

The services of Major Savage being indispensable to the commissioners, it was decided that the expedition would be under the command of Captain Boling. In making this announcement, the major said he expected Ten-ie-ya and his people would come in with us if he was formally invited and a sufficient escort provided. Captain Boling very seriously assured the major that if the Yosemites accepted the invitation, he should endeavor to make the trip a *secure* one; there should be no neglect on the part of the escort if suitable *supplies* were provided for subsistence. Major Savage laughingly replied that as the expedition would be under the especial command of Captain Boling, he had no fears that ample supplies would not be provided.

Our preparations being made, we again started for the Merced in search of the Yosemites. It was the design of Captain Boling to surprise the Indians, if possible, and if not, to cut off the escape of their women and children, the capture of whom would soon bring the warriors to terms. With this plan in view, and leaving Chandler virtually in command of the column, we made a rapid march direct for their valley, crossing the streams without much difficulty, and without accident.

The advance, consisting of Captain Boling with a small detachment, and some of the scouts, quietly entered the valley,* but no Indians were seen. A few new wigwams had been built on the south side near the lower ford, to better guard the entrance as was supposed. Without halting, except to glance at the vacant huts, the advance rode rap-

*On May 9, 1851.

idly on, following a trail up the south side, which our Po-ho-no-chee guide informed the captain was a good trail.

On entering the valley and seeing the deserted wigwams I reached the conclusion that our approach had been heralded. As my military ardor subsided, my enthusiastic love of the beautiful returned to me, and I halted a moment to take a general view of the scenery; intending also to direct the column up the south side. While waiting for Chandler, I examined the huts, and found several bushels of scorched acorns that had been divested of their covering, as if for transportation. I knew that the natives had no more fondness for burnt acorns than Yankees have for burnt beans, and the interpreter Sandino, who was with me at this moment, muttered in Indian Spanish, "Yosemite very poor—no got much eat; acorns, fire burn—pull 'em out." In one of the huts we found a young dog, a miserable cur that barked his affright at our approach, and fled into the brush near by. I told Lieutenant Chandler of the directions left for his guidance, and as he expressed his intention to bring up the rear of the column into closer order, I received permission to move slowly on with his advance, consisting of Firebaugh, Spencer, French, Fisher, Stone, a few others and myself. We were soon overtaken by Chandler, who had given his orders to the rear guard. As we rode along I reported the conclusions of Sandino and my knowledge of the fact that nearly all the acorns had been burnt. I also told him what Sandino had previously said, that the Indians took the shells off the acorns they carried over the mountains, and from this cause, thought the hulled acorns found were designed for a distant transportation. Again referring the matter to Sandino, who was called up for the purpose, he said, "No fire when take off skin; no like 'em; Yosemite close by, want 'em acorn." Upon telling Chandler that Sandino's opinion was that the acorns found were saved from some of the burning supplies fired at our first visit, and that the Yosemites were transporting them to some mountain retreat, the lieutenant could not credit it, and said that "Sandino's opinions are unreliable."

Sandino was not popular, either with our officers or with the "boys." Captain Boling doubted his integrity, while Chandler said he was a most arrant coward and afraid of the wild Indians. Chandler was right; but, nevertheless, Sandino told us many truths. At times his timidity and superstition were very annoying; but if reproved, he became the more confused, and said that many questions made his head ache; *a very common answer to one in search of knowledge among Indians.* Sandino had been sent along by the major as our interpreter, but a Spanish interpreter was necessary to make him of any use. As a scout he was inferior—almost useless. We afterwards found that Sandino's surmises were true. It was evident that the fire had been extinguished at some of the large heaps, and many acorns saved, though in a damaged condition.

As we rode on up the valley, I became more observant of the scenery than watchful for signs, when suddenly my attention was attracted by shadowy objects flitting past rocks and trees on the north side, some distance above El Capitan. Halting, I caught a glimpse of Indians as they passed an open space opposite to us. Seeing that they were discovered, they made no further efforts to hide their movements, but came out into open view, at long rifle range. There were five of them. They saluted us with taunting gestures, and fearlessly kept pace with us as we resumed our march. The river was here a foaming, impassable torrent. The warriors looked with great indifference on our repeated efforts to discover a fording place. As we approached a stretch of comparatively smooth water, I made known to Chandler my intention of swimming the stream to capture them. His answer was: "Bully for you,

Doc; take 'em, if you can, alive, but take 'em *anyhow.*" I
started with Spencer, Firebaugh, French, young Stone and
two others, for a sloping bank where our animals would
most willingly enter the stream; but Stone spurred past
me as we reached the bank, and when Firebaugh's mulish
mustang refused the water, though given the spur, and all
the other mules refused to leave the horse, Stone backed
his mule over the bank, and we swam our mules after the
"boy leader" across the Merced.

The Indians, alarmed by this unexpected movement, fled
up the valley at the top of their speed. By the time we
had crossed, they had nearly reached a bend in the river
above on the north side. We followed at our best gait, but
found the trail obstructed by a mass of what then appeared
to be recently fallen rocks. Without hesitation, we abandoned our mules, and continued the pursuit on foot, up to
the rocky spur known as the "Three Brothers," where
entering the Talus, they disappeared. Find them we could
not. The obstructing rocks on the old north side trail were
known as "We-äck," "The Rocks," and understood to
mean the "fallen rocks," because, according to traditions
they had fallen *upon* the old trail. The modern trail for
horses crossed the stream a short distance below, where
there was a very good ford in a lower stage of water, but at
this time, the early part of May, the volume of water rushing down the Merced was astonishing. We had crossed
readily enough in the heat of excitement; but it was with
feelings of reluctance that we re-entered the cold water
and swam our mules back to where a few of our comrades
had halted on the south side.

Mr. Firebaugh, having failed to get his mustang to follow us, had run him up on the south side as if to cut off the
fugitives, and saw them hide behind a ledge of rocks.

When informed of the situation, Capt. Boling crossed to the north side and came down to the ledge where the scouts were hidden; but the captain could scarcely at first credit Firebaugh's statement that he had seen them climb up the cliff. Our Indian scouts were sent up to hunt out the hidden warriors, and through the means of fair promises, if they came down voluntarily, Captain Boling succeeded in bringing in the five Indians. Three of the captives were known to us, being sons of Ten-ie-ya, one of whom was afterwards killed; the other two were young braves, the wife of one being a daughter of the old chief. The Indian name for the three rocky peaks near which this capture was made was not then known to any of our battalion, but from the strange coincidence of three brothers being made prisoners so near them, we designated the peaks as the

THE THREE BROTHERS.

"Three Brothers." I soon learned that they were called by the Indians "Kom-po-pai-zes," from a fancied resemblance of the peaks to the heads of frogs when sitting up *ready to leap*. A fanciful interpretation has been given the Indian name as meaning "mountains playing leap-frog," but a literal translation is not desirable.

WHILE Captain Boling was engaged in capturing the Indians we had "treed" on the north side of the valley, scouting parties were sent out by Lieutenant Chandler. They spread over the valley, and search was made in every locality that was accessible. Discovering fresh signs on a trail I had unsuccessfully followed on my first visit, I pursued the traces up to a short distance below Mirror Lake. Being alone, I divided my attention between the wonders of the scenery and the tracks I was following, when suddenly I was aroused by discovering a basket of acorns lying by the trail. Seeing that it was a common carrying basket, such as was generally used by the squaws in "packing," I at first came to the conclusion that it had been thrown off by some affrighted squaw in her haste to escape on my approach. Observing another on a trail leading toward the Talus, I felt confident that I had discovered the key to the hiding-place of the Indians we were in search of. Securing my mule with the "riata" I continued the search, and found several baskets before reaching the walls of the cliff, up which, in a kind of groove, the trail ascended. By this time I Legan to be suspicious, and thought that there was too much method in this distribution of acorns along the trail for frightened squaws to have made, and it now occurred to me what Sandino had said of acorns being hulled for transportation up the cliffs; and these *had not been hulled!*

Before reaching the Talus, I observed that the footprints were large, and had been made by the males, as the toes did not turn in, as was usual with the squaws; and it now began to appear to me that the acorns were only left to lead us into some trap; for I was aware that "warriors" seldom disgraced themselves by "packing," like squaws. Taking a look about me, I began to feel that I was venturing too far; my ambitious desire for further investigation vanished, and I hastened back down the trail. While descending, I met Lieutenant Gilbert of C Company, with a few men. They, too, had discovered baskets, dropped by the *"scared Indians,"* and were rushing up in hot pursuit, nearly *capturing* me. I related my discoveries, and told the lieutenant of my suspicions, advising him not to be too hasty in following up the *"lead."* After I had pointed out some of the peculiarities of the location above us, he said with a sigh of disappointment, "By George! Doc, I believe you are right—you are more of an Indian than I am any way; I reckon we had better report this to the captain before we go any further." I replied, "I am now going in to report this strategy to Captain Boling, for I believe he can make some flank movement and secure the Indians, without our being caught in this trap." But while we were descending to the trail, I seriously thought and believed, that Lieutenant Gilbert and his men as well as myself, had had a narrow escape. The bit of history of the rear guard of Charlemagne being destroyed by the Pyrenians flashed through my mind, and I could readily see how destructive such an attack might become.

After taking the precaution to secrete the baskets on the main trail, Lieutenant Gilbert, with his scouts, continued his explorations in other localities, saying as he left that he would warn all whom he might see "not to get into the trap." I mounted my mule and rode down the valley in search of Captain Boling, and found him in an oak grove near our old camp, opposite a cliff, now known as "Hammo'' (the lost arrow). I here learned the particulars of his successful capture of the five scouts of Ten-ie-ya's band, and at his request asked them, through Sandino, who had come over with the *"kitchen mules,"* why they had so exposed themselves to our view. They replied that Ten-ie-ya knew of our approach before we reached the valley. That by his orders they were sent to watch our movements and report to him. That they did not think we could cross the Merced with our horses until we reached the upper fords; and therefore, when discovered, did not fear. They said that Ten-ie-ya would come in and "have a talk with the white chief when he knows we are here."

After repeated questioning as to where their people were, and where the old chief would be found if a messenger should be sent to him, they gave us to understand that they were to meet Ten-ie-ya near To-co-ya, at the same time pointing in the direction of the "North Dome." Captain Boling assured them that if Ten-ie-ya would come in with his people he could do so with safety. That he desired to make peace with him, and did not wish to injure any of them. The young brave was the principal spokesman, and he replied: "Ten-ie-ya will come in when he hears what has been said to us."

Having acquired all the information it was possible to get from the Indians, Captain Boling said that in the morning he would send a messenger to the old chief and see if he would come in. When told this the young "brave" appeared to be very anxious to be permitted to go after him, saying: "He is there now," pointing towards the "North Dome," "another day he will be on the 'Skye Mountains,' or anywhere," meaning that his movements were uncertain.

Captain Boling had so much confidence in his statements

that he decided to send some of the scouts to the region of the North Dome for Ten-ie-ya; but all efforts of our allies and of ourselves failed to obtain any further clue to Ten-ie-ya's hiding-place, for the captives said that they dare not disclose their signals or countersign, for the penalty was death, and none other would be answered or understood by their people. I here broke in upon the captain's efforts to obtain *useful knowledge* from his prisoners, by telling him of the discovery of baskets of acorns found on the trail; and gave him my reasons for believing it to be a design to lead us into an ambush—that the Indians were probably on the cliff above. I volunteered the suggestion that a movement in that direction would surprise them while watching the trap set for us.

Captain Boling replied: "It is too late in the day for a job of that kind; we will wait and see if Ten-ie-ya will come in. I have made up my mind to send two of our prisoners after him, and keep the others as hostages until he comes. To make a sure thing of this, doctor, I want you to take these two," pointing to one of the sons and the son-in-law of Ten-ie-ya, "and go with them to the place where they have said a trail leads up the cliff to Ten-ie-ya's hiding-place. You will take care that they are not molested by any of our boys while on this trip. Take any one with you in camp, if you do not care to go alone."

Taking a small lunch to break my fast since the morning meal, I concluded to make the trip on foot; my mule having been turned loose with the herd. Arming myself, I started alone with the two prisoners which Capt. Boling had consigned to my guardianship. I kept them ahead of me on the trail, as I always did when traveling with any of that race. We passed along the westerly base of the North

Dome at a rapid gait, without meeting any of my comrades, and had reached a short turn in the trail around a
point of rocks, when the Indians suddenly sprang back and
jumped behind me. From their frightened manner, and
cry of terror, I was not apprehensive of any treachery on
their part. Involuntarily I cried out, "Hallo! what's up
now?" and stepped forward to see what had so alarmed
them. Before me stood George Fisher with his rifle lev-
eled at us. I instantly said: "Hold on, George! these
Indians are under my care!" He determinedly exclaimed
without change of position, "Get out of the way, doctor,
those Indians have got to die." Just behind Fisher was
Sergeant Cameron, with a man on his shoulders. As he
hastily laid him on the ground, I was near enough to see
that his clothing was soiled and badly torn, and that his
face, hands and feet were covered with blood. His eyes
were glazed and bloodshot, and it was but too evident that
he had been seriously injured. From the near proximity
of the basket trail, I instantly surmised they had been on
the cliff above. The scene was one I shall long remember.

It seemed but a single motion for Cameron to deposit his
burden and level his rifle. He ordered me to stand aside
if I valued my own safety. I replied as quietly as I could,
"Hold on, boys! Captain Boling sent me to guard these
Indians from harm, and I shall obey orders." I motioned
the Indians to keep to my back or they would be killed.
Cameron shouted: "They have almost killed Spencer, and
have got to die." As he attempted to get sight, he said:
"Give way, Bunnell, I don't want to hurt you." This I
thought *very condescending*, and I replied with emphasis:
"These Indians are under my charge, and I shall protect
them. If you shoot you commit murder." The whole

transaction thus far seemingly occupied but a moment's time, when to the surprise of us all, Spencer called my name. I moved forward a little, and said to them, "Throw up your rifles and let me come in to see Spencer." "Come in! *you* are safe," replied Fisher—still watching the Indians with a fierce determination in his manner. Spencer raised himself in a sitting position, and at a glance seemed to take in the situation of affairs, for he said: "Bunnell is right; boys, don't shoot; mine is but the fortune of war;" and telling Cameron to call me, he again seemed to fall partly into stupor. As I again moved towards them with the Indians behind me, they with some reluctance, put up their rifles. Fisher turned his back to me as he said with sarcasm, "Come in with your friends, doctor, and thank Spencer for their safety." They relieved their excitement with volleys of imprecations. Cameron said that I "was a —— sight too high-toned to suit friends that had always been willing to stand by me."

This occurrence did not destroy good feeling toward each other, for we were all good friends after the excitement had passed over.

I examined Spencer and found that, although no bones were broken, he was seriously bruised and prostrated by the shock induced by his injuries. Fisher started for camp to bring up a horse or mule to carry Spencer in. I learned that they had fallen into the trap on the "basket trail," and that Spencer had been injured while ascending the cliff as I had suspected. He had, unfortunately, been *trailed in,* as I had been. The particulars Cameron related to me and in my hearing after we had arrived in camp. As the Indians represented to me that the trail they proposed to take up the cliff was but a little way up the north branch, I concluded to go on with them, and then be back in time to accompany Spencer into camp. Speaking some cheering words to Spencer, I turned to leave, when Cameron said to him: "You ain't dead yet, my boy." Spencer held out his hand, and as he took it Cameron said, with visible emotion, but emphatic declaration: "We will pay them back for this if the chance ever comes; Doc. is decidedly too conscientious in this affair." I escorted the Indians some way above "Mirror Lake," where they left the trail and commenced to climb the cliff.

On my return I found that Cameron had already started with Spencer; I soon overtook them and relieved him of his burden, and from there carried Spencer into camp. We found Fisher vainly trying to catch his mule. The most of the horses were still out with the scouts, and all animals in camp had been turned loose. Sergeant Cameron, while Fisher was assisting me in the removal of Spencer's clothing and dressing his wounds, had prepared a very comfortable bed, made of boughs, that the kind-hearted boys thoughtfully brought in; and after he was made comfortable and nourishment given him, the sergeant related to Captain Boling the details of their adventure.

After supper, the explorers having all come in, the boys gathered around the sergeant and importuned him to give the history of his adventures. After reflectively bringing up the scene to view, he began: "We got into mighty close quarters! Come to think of it, I don't see how we happened to let ourselves be caught in that dead-fall. I reckon we must have fooled ourselves some. The way of it was this: We went up on the south side as far as we could ride, and after rummaging around for awhile, without finding anything, Spencer wanted to go up the North Cañon and get a good look at that mountain with one side split off; so I told the boys to look about for themselves, as there were no Indians in the valley. Some of them went on up the South

Cañon, and the rest of us went over to the North Cañon. After crossing the upper ford, Spencer and I concluded to walk up the cañon, so we sent our animals down to graze with the herd. Spencer looked a good long while at that split mountain, and called it a 'half dome.' I concluded he might name it what he liked, if he would leave it and go to camp; for I was getting tired and hungry and said so. Spencer said 'All right, we'll go to camp.'

"On our way down, as we passed that looking-glass pond, he wanted to take one more look, and told me to go ahead and he'd soon overtake me; but that I wouldn't do, so he said: 'No matter, then; I can come up some other time.' As we came on down the trail below the pond, I saw some acorns scattered by the side of the trail, and told Spencer there were Indians not far off. After looking about for awhile Spencer found a basket nearly full behind some rocks, and in a little while discovered a trail leading up towards the cliff. We followed this up a piece, and soon found several baskets of acorns. I forgot about being hungry, and after talking the matter over we decided to make a sort of reconnoissance before we came in to make any report. Well, we started on up among the rocks until we got to a mighty steep place, a kind of gulch that now looked as if it had been scooped out for a stone battery. The trail up it was as steep as the roof on a meeting-house, and worn so slippery that we couldn't get a foothold. I wanted to see what there was above, and took off my boots and started up. Spencer did the same and followed me. I had just got to the swell of the steepest slope, where a crack runs across the face of the wall, and was looking back to see if Spencer would make the riffle, when I heard a crash above me, and saw a rock as big as a hogshead rolling down the cliff toward us. I sprang on up behind a rock that happened to be in the right place, for there was no time to hunt for any other shelter.

"I had barely reached cover when the bounding rock struck with a crash by my side, and bounded clear over Spencer, who had run across the crevice and was stooping down and steadying himself with his rifle. A piece of the big rock that was shattered into fragments and thrown in all directions, struck his rifle out of his hands, and sent him whirling and clutching down a wall fifty feet. He lodged out of sight, where in going up we had kicked off our leathers. I thought he was killed, for he did not answer when I called, and I had no chance then to go to him, for a tremendous shower of stones came rushing by me. I expected he would be terribly mangled at first, but soon noticed that the swell in the trail caused the rocks to bound clear over him onto the rocks in the valley. I looked up to see where they came from just as an Indian stuck his head above a rock. My rifle came up of its own accord. It was a quick sight, but with me they are generally the best, and as I fired that Indian jumped into the air with a yell and fell back onto the ledge. He was hit, I know, and I reckon *he went west*. Every rock above was soon a yelling as if alive. As I expected another discharge from their stone artillery, I slid down the trail, picked up Spencer, and 'vamoused the ranche,' just as they fired another shot of rocks down after us. I did not stay to see where they struck after I was out of range, for my rifle and Spencer took about all of my attention until safely down over the rocks. While I was there resting for a moment, Fisher came up the trail. He heard me fire and had heard the rocks tumbling down the cliff. Thinking someone was in trouble, he was going to find out who it was.

"We concluded at first that Spencer was done for, for his heart beat very slow and he was quite dumpish. We had just started for camp with him, and met Bunnell going out with the two Indians. I reckon we would have sent them on a trip down where it is warmer than up there on the mountains, if Spencer hadn't roused himself just then. He stopped the game. He called for the doctor; but Bunnell was as stubborn as Firebaugh's mustang and would not leave the Indians. We had to let them pass, before he would take a look at Spencer. Doc. is generally all right enough, but he was in poor business today. When I told him it was his own messmate, he said it didn't matter if it were his own brother. If Captain Boling will make a shooting match and put up the other three, I'll give my horse for the first three shots. Shooting will be cheap after that.''

I have given the substance only of Sergeant Cameron's talk to the group around him, though but poorly imitating his style, in order to show the feeling that was aroused by Spencer's misfortune. Spencer's uniformly quiet and gentlemanly manners made no enemies among rough comrades, who admired the courageous hardihood of ''the little fellow,'' and respected him as a man. Many expressions of sympathy were given by the scouts who gathered around our tent, on learning of his injury. For some days after the event, he could scarcely be recognized, his face was so swollen and discolored. But what Spencer seemed most to regret was the injury to his feet and knees, which had been cruelly rasped by the coarse granite in his descent.

The injury from this cause was so great that he was unable to make those explorations that footmen alone could accomplish. He was an enthusiastic lover of nature, an accomplished scholar and man of the world. Having spent five years in France and Germany in the study of modern languages, after having acquired a high standing here in Latin and Greek.

We thought him peculiarly gifted, and hoped for something from his pen descriptive of the Yosemite that would endure; but he could never be induced to make any effort to describe any feature of the valley, saying: "That fools only rush in where wise men stand in awe." We were bedfellows and friends, and from this cause chiefly, perhaps, all the incidents of his accident were strongly impressed on my memory. After his full recovery his feet remained tender for a long time, and he made but one extended exploration after his accident while in the battalion.

During the camp discussion regarding my course in sav-

INDIAN PASS

ing the two captives, Captain Boling and myself were amused listeners. No great pains were taken as a rule to hide one's light under a bushel, and we were sitting not far off. The captain said that he now comprehended the extreme anxiety of the captives to see Ten-ie-ya, as doubtless they knew of his intentions to roll rocks down on any who attempted to follow up that trail; and probably supposed we would kill them if any of us were killed. As he left our tent he remarked: "These hostages will have to stay in camp. They will not be safe outside of it, if some of the boys chance to get their eyes on them."

ALTHOUGH our camp was undisturbed during the night, no doubt we were watched from the adjacent cliffs, as in fact all our movements were. The captives silently occupied the places by the camp-fire. They were aware of Spencer's mishap, and probably expected their lives might be forfeited; for they could see but little sympathy in the countenances of those about them. The reckless demonstrations of the more frolicksome boys were watched with anxious uncertainty. The sombre expressions and *energetic* remarks of the sympathizers of Spencer induced Captain Boling to have a special guard detailed from those who were not supposed to be prejudiced against the Indians, as it was deemed all-important to the success of the campaign that Ten-ie-ya should be conciliated or captured; therefore, this detail was designed as much for the protection of the hostages as to prevent their escape. The messengers had assured the captain that Ten-ie-ya would be in before noon, but the hostages told Sandino that possibly the messengers might not find him near To-co-ya, where they expected to meet him, as he might go a long distance away into the mountains before they would again see him. They evidently supposed that the chief, like themselves, had become alarmed at the failure of his plan to draw us into ambush, and had fled farther into the Sierras; or else doubted his coming at all, and wished to encourage the captain to hope for the coming of Ten-ie-ya that their own chances of escape might be improved.

Sandino professed to believe their statement, telling me that they—the five prisoners—expected to have trailed us up to the scene of Spencer's disaster; failing in which— owing to our having forced them to hide near the "Frog Mountains"—they still expected to meet him on the cliff where the rocks had been rolled down, and not at To-co-ya. In this conversation, the fact appeared—derived as he said indirectly from conversations with the prisoners—that there were projecting ledges and slopes extending along the cliff on the east side of Le-hamite to To-co-ya, where Indians could pass and re-pass, undiscovered, and all of our movements could be watched. The substance of this communication I gave to Captain Boling, but it was discredited as an impossibility; and he expressed the belief that the old chief would make his appearance by the hour agreed upon with his messengers, designated by their pointing to where the sun would be on his arrival in camp. Accordingly the captain gave orders that no scouts would be sent out until after that time. Permission, however, was given to those who desired to leave camp for their own pleasure or diversion.

A few took advantage of this opportunity and made excursions up the North Cañon to the "basket trail," with a view of examining that locality, and at the same time indulging their curiosity to see the place where Cameron and Spencer had been trailed in and entrapped by the Indians. Most of the command preferred to remain in camp to repair damages, rest, and to amuse themselves in a general way. Among the recreations indulged in was shooting at a target with the bows and arrows taken from the captured Indians. The bow and arrows of the young brave were superior to those of the others, both in material and workmanship. Out of curiosity some of the boys induced him to give a specimen of his skill. His shots were really commendable. The readiness with which he handled his weapons excited the admiration of the lookers-on. He, with apparent ease, flexed a bow which many of our men could not bend without great effort, and whose shots were as liable to endanger the camp as to hit the target. This trial of skill was witnessed by Captain Boling and permitted, as no trouble was anticipated from it.

After this exercise had ceased to be amusing, and the most of those in camp had their attention engaged in other matters, the guard, out of curiosity and for pastime, put up the target at long range. To continue the sport it was necessary to bring in the arrows used, and as it was difficult to find them, an Indian was taken along to aid in the search. The young brave made a more extended shot than all others. With great earnestness he watched the arrow, and started with one of the guard, who was unarmed, to find it. While pretending to hunt for the "lost arrow," he made a dash from the guard toward "Indian Cañon," and darted into the rocky Talus, which here encroached upon the valley. The guard on duty hearing the alarm of his comrade and seeing the Indian at full speed, fired at him, but without effect, as the intervening rocks and the zig-zag course he was running made the shot a difficult one, without danger of hitting his comrade, who was following in close pursuit.

This aggravating incident greatly annoyed Captain Boling, who was peculiarly sensitive on the subject of escaped prisoners. The verdant guard was reprimanded in terms more expressive than polite; and relieved from duty. The remaining Indians were then transferred to the special care of Lieutenant Chandler, who was told by Captain Boling to "keep them secure if it took the whole command to do it." The Indians were secured by being tied back to back, with a "riata" or picket rope, and then fastened to an oak tree in the middle of the camp, and the guard—a new one—stationed where they could constantly watch. The morning passed, and the hour of ten arrived, without Ten-ie-ya. Captain Boling then sent out Sandino and the scouts to hunt for him, and if found, to notify him that he was expected. Sandino soon came back, and reported that he had seen Ten-ie-ya and talked with him; but that he was unable to reach him from below, on account of the steepness of the ledge. Sandino reported that Ten-ie-ya was unwilling to come in. That he expressed a determination not to go to the Fresno. He would make peace with the white chief if he would be allowed to remain in his own territory. Neither he nor his people would go to the valley while the white men were there. They would stay on the mountains or go to the Monos.

When this was communicated to Captain Boling, he gave orders for a select number of scouts to make an effort to bring in the old malcontent, *alive, if possible.* Lieutenant Chandler, therefore, with a few Noot-chü and Po-ho-no-chee scouts, to climb above the projecting ledge, and a few of our men to cut off retreat, started up the Ten-ie-ya branch, led by Sandino as guide. After passing the "Royal Arches," Sandino let Chandler understand that he and his scouts had best go up by the Wai-ack or Mirror Lake trail, in order to cut off Ten-ie-ya's retreat; while he went back to the rock he pointed out as the place where he had seen and talked with Ten-ie-ya; and which commanded a view of our camp. This was distasteful to Chandler; but after a moment's reflection said: "Let the converted knave go back to camp; I'll act without him, and catch the old chief if he is on the mountain, and that without resorting to Indian treachery.''

While in camp Sandino had seemed to convey some message to the hostages, and when asked the purport of it had answered evasively. This had prejudiced Chandler, but it had not surprised me, nor did it appear inconsistent with Sandino's loyalty to Captain Boling; but the Indian was unpopular. As to his code of honor and his morality, it was about what should have been expected of one in his position, and as a frequent interpreter of his interpretations and sayings, I finally told the captain and Chandler that it would be best to take Sandino for what he might be worth; as continued doubt of him could not be disguised, and would tend to make a knave or fool of him. On one occasion he was so alarmed by some cross looks and words given him, that he fell upon his knees and begged for his life, thinking, as he said afterward, that he was to be killed.

During the night, and most of the time during the day, I was engaged in attendance on Spencer. Doctor Black understood it to be Spencer's wish that I should treat him. I gave but little attention to other matters, although I could see from our tent everything that was going on in camp. Not long after the departure of Chandler and his scouts, as I was about leaving camp in search of balsam of fir and other medicinals, I observed one of the guard watching the prisoners with a pleased and self-satisfied expression. As I glanced toward the Indians I saw that they were endeavoring to untie each other, and said to two of the detail as I passed them, ''That ought to be reported to the officer of the guard. They should be separated, and not allowed to tempt their fate.'' I was told that it was ''already known to the officers.'' I was then asked if I was on guard duty. The significance of this I was fully able to interpret, and passed on to the vicinity of ''The High Falls.''

On my return an hour afterwards, I noticed when nearing camp that the Indians were gone from the tree to which they were tied when I left. Supposing that they had probably been removed for greater security, I gave it no further thought until, without any intimation of what had occurred during my short absence, I saw before me the dead body of old Ten-ie-ya's youngest son, the warm blood still oozing from a wound in his back. He was lying just outside of our camp, within pistol range of the tree to which he had been tied.

I now comprehended the action of the guard. I learned that the other Indian had been fired at, but had succeeded in making his escape over the same ground and into the cañon where the other brave had disappeared. I found on expressing my unqualified condemnation of this cowardly act, that I was not the only one to denounce it. It was a cause of regret to nearly the whole command. Instead of the praise expected by the guard for the dastardly manner in which the young Indian was killed, they were told by Captain Boling that they had committed murder. Sergeant Cameron was no lover of Indians, but for this act his boiling wrath could hardly find vent, even when aided by some red-hot expressions. I learned, to my extreme mortification, that no report had been made to any of the officers. The Indians had been permitted to untie themselves, and an opportunity had been given them to attempt to escape in order to fire upon them, expecting to kill them both; and only that a bullet-pouch had been hung upon the muzzle of one of the guard's rifles while leaning against a tree (for neither were on duty at the moment), no doubt both of the captives would have been killed.

Upon investigation, it was found that the fatal shot had been fired by a young man who had been led by an old Texan sinner to think that killing Indians or Mexicans was a duty; and surprised at Captain Boling's view of his conduct, declared with an injured air, that he "would not kill another Indian if the woods were full of them." Although no punishment was ever inflicted upon the perpetrators of the act, they were both soon sent to coventry, and feeling their disgrace, were allowed to do duty with the pack-train. Captain Boling had, before the occurrence of this incident, decided to establish his permanent camp on the south side of the Merced. The location selected was near the bank of the river, in full view of, and nearly opposite "The Fall." This camp was headquarters during our stay in the valley, which was extended to a much longer time than we had anticipated. Owing to several mountain storms, our stay was prolonged over a month. The bottoms, or meadow land, afforded good grazing for our animals, and we were there more conveniently reached by our couriers and supply trains from the Fresno.

From this point our excursions were made. All Indians attach great importance to securing the bodies of their dead for appropriate ceremonials, which with these was "cremation." They with others of the mountain tribes in this part of California, practiced the burning of their dead in accordance with their belief in a future state of existence, which was that if the body was burned, the spirit was released and went to "the happy land in the west." If this ceremony was omitted, the spirit haunted the vicinity, to the annoyance of the friends as well as the enemies of the deceased. Knowing this, Captain Boling felt a desire to make some atonement for the unfortunate killing of the son of Ten-ie-ya, the chief of the tribe with whom he was endeavoring to "make peace," and therefore made his arrangements to take advantage of this custom to propitiate the Indians by giving them an opportunity to remove

THE YOSEMITE FALLS.

the body of the youth. Accordingly, the order was at once given to break camp.

While the pack animals were being loaded, Lieutenant Chandler with his party brought in Ten-ie-ya. The Indian scouts, who were first sent out with Sandino and who knew where the talk with the chief had been held, passed on in advance and saw that he was still at his perch, watching the movements below him. Some of those out on leave discovered him also, seated on a ledge that appeared only accessible from above. The Po-ho-no-chee scouts, thinking to capture him by cutting off his retreat, followed an upper trail and reached the summit of the wall, while a few of Chandler's men, who were apprized of the situation by some of the pleasure-seekers whom they met, took a lower trail, and thus were in advance of the Indian scouts when Ten-ie-ya's retreat was reached. To their disappointment, the old chief could not be found, though at intervals fresh signs and heaps of stones were seen along the southwestern slope of the mountain.

The sequel to the disappearance of Ten-ie-ya, as explained by Sandino, was simply as follows: When sent back by Chandler, Sandino resolved to make another effort to induce Ten-ie-ya to come in, lest Chandler should kill him if found. Accordingly he again climbed to the foot of the old chief's perch, and was talking with him, when some small loose stones came rolling down towards them. Seeing that his retreat above had been cut off, Ten-ie-ya at first ran along westerly, on the slope of the mountain towards Indian Cañon; but finding that he was cut off in that direction also, by the Neut-chü and Po-ho-no-chee scouts, he turned and came down a trail through an oak tree-top to the valley, which Sandino had by this time reached, and where he had been attracted by the noise made in the pursuit. Lieutenant Chandler had not climbed up the trail, and hearing

Sandino's cry for help, and the noise above him, he was able to reach the place when Ten-ie-ya descended, in time to secure him. Ten-ie-ya said the men above him were rolling stones down, and he did not like to go up, as they broke and flew everywhere; for that reason he came down.

Ten-ie-ya accompanied his captors without making any resistance, although he strongly censured the Indians for being instrumental in his capture. They did not reach the valley in time to take part in the capture, but as Ten-ie-ya had said: "It was their cunning that had discovered the way to his hiding place."

None of the party of explorers or those under Chandler were aware of the event that had occurred during their absence. As Ten-ie-ya walked toward the camp, proudly conscious of being an object of attention from us, his eye fell upon the dead body of his favorite son, which still lay where he had fallen, without having been disturbed. He halted for a moment, without visible emotion, except a slight quivering of his lips. As he raised his head, the index to his feelings was exhibited in the glaring expression of deadly hate with which he gazed at Captain Boling, and cast his eyes over the camp as if in search of the remains of the other son, the fellow captive of the one before him. Captain Boling expressed his regret of the occurrence, and had the circumstances explained to him, but not a single word would he utter in reply; not a sound escaped his compressed lips. He passively accompanied us to our camp on the south side of the river. It was evident that every movement of ours was closely scrutinized. Sandino was instructed to notify the chief that the body could be taken away. This permission was also received in silence.

Upon riding over to the camp ground the next morning, it was found that the body had been carried up or secreted in Indian Cañon, as all of the tracks led that way. This ravine became known to *us* as "Indian Cañon," though called by the Indians "Le-Hamite," "the arrow-wood." It was also known to them by the name of "Scho-tal-lo-wi," meaning the way to *"Fall Creek."* The rocks near which we were encamped, between "Indian Cañon" and "The Falls," were now called by the Po-ho-no-chee scouts who were with us, "Hammo," or "Ummo," "The Lost Arrow," in commemoration of the event. On the morning following the capture of Ten-ie-ya, Captain Boling tried to have a talk with him; but he would not reply to a question asked through the interpreter; neither would he converse with Sandino or the Indians with us. He maintained this moody silence and extreme taciturnity for several days afterwards.

Finding that nothing could be accomplished through the old chief, Captain Boling gave orders to re-commence our search for his people. Scouting parties were started on foot to explore as far as was practicable on account of the snow. Although it was now May, the snow prevented a very extended search in the higher Sierras. On the first day out these parties found that, although they had made a faithful and active search, they had not performed half they had planned to do when starting. Distances were invariably underestimated. This we afterward found was the case in all of our excursions in the mountains, where we estimated distance by the eye; and calling attention to the phenomena, I tried to have the principle applied to heights as well. The height of the mountainous cliffs, and the clear atmosphere made objects appear near, but the time taken to reach them convinced us that our eyes had deceived us in our judgment of distance. To avoid the severe labor that was imposed upon us by carrying our provisions and blankets, an attempt was made to use pack-mules, but the circuitous route we were compelled to take consumed too much time; besides the ground we were desir-

ous of going over was either too soft and yielding, or too
rocky and precipitous. We were compelled to leave the
mules and continue our explorations on foot. Later in the
season there would have been no difficulty in exploring the
mountains on horseback, if certain well established routes
and passes were kept in view; but aside from these our
Indian guides could give us little or no information. This
we accounted for upon the theory that, as there was no
game of consequence in the higher Sierras, and the cold
was great as compared with the lower altitudes, the Indians'
knowledge of the "Higher Sierras" was only acquired
while passing over them, or while concealed in them from
the pursuit of their enemies. All scouting parties were,
therefore, principally dependent upon their own resources,
and took with them a supply of food and their blankets for
a bivouac. In this way much time and fatigue of travel
was saved. Some were more adventurous than others in
their explorations. These, on returning from a scout of
one or more days out, would come in ragged and foot-sore,
and report with enthusiasm their adventures, and the wonders they had seen. Their descriptions around the camp-
fire at night were at first quite exciting; but a few nights'
experience in the vicinity of the snow line, without finding
Indians, soon cooled down the ardor of all but a very few,
who, from their persistent wandering explorations, were
considered somewhat eccentric.

Through our Indian scouts we learned that some of the
Yosemites had gone to the Tuolumne. These were Tuolumne
Indians, who had intermarried with the Yosemites, and
had been considered as a part of Ten-ie-ya's band. Taking
their women and children, they returned to the Tuolumne
tribe as soon as it was known that Ten-ie-ya had been captured; fearing he would again promise to take his band to
the Fresno. Our orders prohibited us from disturbing the

Tuolumne Indians; we therefore permitted them to return to their allegiance without attempting to follow them.

Ten-ie-ya was treated with kindness, and as his sorrow for the loss of his son seemed to abate, he promised to call in some of his people, and abide by their decision, when they had heard the statements of Captain Boling. At night he would call as if to some one afar off. He said his people were not far from our camp and could hear his voice. We never heard a reply, although the calls were continued by order of Captain Boling for many nights.

Although he was closely watched by the camp guard, he made an attempt to escape while the guard's back was momentarily turned upon him. Sergeant Cameron, who had especial charge of him at the time, saw his movement, and as he rushed from his keeper, Cameron dashed after and caught him before he was able to plunge into and swim the river.

As Ten-ie-ya was brought into the presence of Captain Boling by Sergeant Cameron, after this attempt to escape, he supposed that he would now be condemned to be shot. With mingled fear of the uncertainty of his life being spared, and his furious passion at being foiled in his attempt to regain his liberty, he forgot his usual reserve and shrewdness. His grief for the loss of his son and the hatred he entertained toward Captain Boling, who he considered as responsible for his death, was uppermost in his thoughts, and without any of his taciturn, diplomatic style he burst forth in lamentations and denunciations, given in a loud voice and in a style of language and manner of delivery which took us all by surprise. In his excitement, he made a correct use of many Spanish words, showing that he was more familiar with them than he had ever admitted even to Sandino; but the more emphatic expressions were such as may often be heard used by the muleteers of Mexico and

South America, but are not found in the Lexicons. As he approached Captain Boling, he began in a highly excited tone: *"Kill me,* sir captain! Yes, *kill me,* as you killed my son; as you would kill my people if they were to come to you! You would kill all my race if you had the power. Yes, sir, American, you can now tell your warriors to kill the old chief; you have made me sorrowful, my life dark; you killed the child of my heart, why not kill the father? But wait a little; when I am dead I will call to my people to come to you, I will call louder than you have had me call; that they shall hear me in their sleep, and come to avenge the death of their chief and his son. Yes, sir, American, my spirit will make trouble for you and your people, as you have caused trouble to me and my people. With the wizards, I will follow the white men and make them fear me." He here aroused himself to a sublime frenzy, and completed his rhapsody by saying: "You may kill me, sir captain, but you shall not live in peace. I will follow in your footsteps, I will not leave my home, but be with the spirits among the rocks, the water-falls, in the rivers and in the winds; wheresoever you go I will be with you. You will not see me, but you will fear the spirit of the old chief, and grow cold.* The great spirits have spoken! I am done."

Captain Boling allowed the old orator to finish his talk without interruption. Although he did not fully understand him, he was amused at his earnest style and impetuous gestures. On hearing it interpreted, he humorously replied: "I comprehended the most of what he said. The old chief has improved. If he was only reliable he would make a better interpreter than Sandino. As for speech-

---

*It is claimed by all Indian "Medicine Men" that the presence of a spirit is announced by a *cool* breeze, and that sometimes they turn cold and shake as with an ague.

making, Doc., I throw up. The old Pow-wow can beat me all hollow.'' Ten-ie-ya earnestly watched the countenance of the good-natured captain, as if to learn his decision in the matter. The captain observing him, quietly said: ''Sergeant Cameron! the old sachem looks hungry, and as it is now about supper time, you had better give him an extra ration or two, and then see that he is so secured that he will not have a chance to escape from us again.''

I watched the old incorrigible while he was delivering this eloquent harangue (which, of course, is necessarily a free translation) with considerable curiosity. Under the excitement of the moment he appeared many years younger. With his vigorous old age he displayed a *latent* power which was before unknown to us. I began to feel a sort of veneration for him. My sympathies had before been aroused for his sorrow, and I now began to have almost a genuine respect for him; but as I passed him half an hour afterwards, the poetry of his life appeared changed. He was regaling himself on fat pork and beans from a wooden dish which had been brought to him by order of Cameron. This he seemed to enjoy with an appetite of a hungry animal. His guard had provided his wooden bowl and ladle by chipping them out of an alder tree, but failing to finish them smoothly, they could not be *properly* washed; but this fact seemed not to disturb his relish for the food. As I looked at his enjoyment of the loaded dish, I now saw only a dirty old Indian. The spiritual man had disappeared. I addressed him in Spanish, but not a word of reply; instead he pointed to his ear, thereby indicating that he was deaf to the language. Afterwards he even repudiated his ''*Medicineship.*''

LOOKING FOR INDIANS ON VALLEY WALLS

A few days after we had moved camp to the south side of the Merced, Captain Boling was prostrated with an attack of pneumonia. From frequent wettings received while crossing the ice-cold torrents, and a too free use of this snow water, which did not agree with many, he had for some days complained of slight illness, but after this attack he was compelled to acknowledge himself sick. Although the severe symptoms continued but a few days, his recovery was lingering, and confined him to camp; consequently he knew but little of his rocky surroundings. Although regular reports were made to him by the scouting parties, he had but an imperfect conception of the labors performed by them in clambering over the rocks of the cañons and mountains. He would smile at the reports the more enthusiastic gave of the wonders discovered; patiently listen to the complaints of the more practical at their want of success in what they termed their futile explorations; and finally concluded to suspend operations until the fast-melting snow had so disappeared from the high mountain passes as to permit our taking a supply train, in order to make our search thorough. The winter had been an unusually dry and cold one—so said the Indians—and, as a consequence, the accumulations of snow in the passes and lake basins had remained almost intact. A succession of mountain storms added to the drifts, so that when the snow finally began to melt, the volume of water coming from the "High Sierras" was simply prodigious—out of all proportion to the quantity that had fallen upon the plains below.

Sandino persisted in trying to make the captain believe that most of the Yosemites had already gone through the Mono Pass, and that those remaining hidden were but the members of Ten-ie-ya's family. This theory was not accepted by Captain Boling, and occasional scouting parties would still be sent out. A few of us continued to make short excursions, more for adventure and to gratify curiosity, than with the expectation of discovering the hiding-places of the Indians, although we kept up the form of a search. We thus became familiar with most of the objects of interest.

The more practical of our command could not remain quiet in camp during this suspension of business. Beside the ordinary routine of camp duties, they engaged in athletic sports and horse racing. A very fair race track was cleared and put in condition, and some of the owners of fast horses were very much surprised to see their favorites trailing behind some of the fleet-footed mules. A maltese Kentucky blooded mule, known as the "Vining Mule," distanced all but one horse in the command, and so pleased was Captain Boling with its gracefully supple movements that he paid Vining* for it a thousand dollars in gold.

For a change of amusement, the members of our "Jockey Club" would mount their animals and take a look at such points of interest as had been designated in our camp-fire conversations as most remarkable. The scenery in the Yosemite and vicinity, which is now familiar to so many, was at that time looked upon with varied degrees of individual curiosity and enjoyment, ranging from the enthusiastic to almost a total indifference to the sublime grandeur presented. It is doubtful if any of us could have given a very graphic description of what we saw, as the impressions then received were so far below the reality. Distance, height, depth and dimensions were invariably underestimated; notwithstanding this, our attempts at descriptions after our return to the settlements, were received as exaggerated "yarns."

While in Mariposa, upon one occasion not very long after the discovery of Yosemite, I was solicited by Wm. T. Whitachre, a newspaper correspondent from San Francisco, to furnish him a written description of the valley. This, of course, was beyond my ability to do; but I disinterestedly complied with his request as far as I could, by giving him some written details to work upon. On reading the paper over, he advised me to reduce my estimates of heights of cliffs and waterfalls, at least fifty per centum, or my judgment would be a subject of ridicule even to my personal

---

*Probably Lee Vining. See also page 173.

friends. I had estimated El Capitan[1] at from fifteen hundred to two thousand feet high; the Yosemite Fall[2] at about fifteen hundred feet, and other prominent points of interest in about the same proportion.

To convince me of my error of judgment, he stated that he had interviewed Captain Boling and some others, and that none had estimated the highest cliffs above a thousand feet. He further said that he would not like to risk his own reputation as a correspondent, without considerable modification of my statements, etc. Feeling outraged at this imputation, I tore up the manuscript, and left the "newspaper man" to obtain where he could such data for his patrons as would please him. It remained for those who came after us to examine scientifically, and to correctly describe what we only observed as wonderful natural curiosities. With but few exceptions, curiosity was gratified by but superficial examination of the objects now so noted. We were aware that the valley was high up in the regions of the Sierra Nevada, but its altitude above the sea level was only guessed at. The heights of its immense granite walls was an uncertainty, and so little real appreciation was there in the battalion, that some never climbed above the Vernal Fall. They know nothing of the beauties of the Nevada Fall, or the "Little Yosemite." We, as a body of men, were aware that the mountains, cañons and waterfalls were on a grandly extensive scale, but of the proportions of that scale we had arrived at no very definite conclusions.

All of the smaller streams that pour their tribute into the valley during the melting of the snow, become later in the season but dry ravines or mere rivulets, but the principal tributaries, running up, as they do, into the lake and snow reservoirs, continue throughout the dry season to pour their

---

[1] Actually 3,609 feet   [2] Actually 2,565 feet.

ample supply. After returning from my mountain explorations, I freely questioned Ten-ie-ya of the places we had visited. The old chief had gradually assumed his customary manner of sociability, and if convinced by outline maps in the sand that we were familiar with a locality, he would become quite communicative, and give the names of the places described in distinct words. Our English alphabet utterly fails to express the sounds of many of them, for they were as unpronounceable as Apache. This difficulty is owing more or less to the guttural termination given by the Indians.

Another important fact which causes a confusion of these names is, that owing to the poverty of their language, they use the same word, or what seems to be the same, for several objects, which by accent, comparison and allusion, or by gestures, are readily understood by them, but which it is difficult for one not familiar with the dialect to comprehend, and still more difficult to illustrate or remember.

"SCENE IN VALLEY OF YOSEMITE, CALIFORNIA", EL CAPITAN (LOOKING WEST)
BY THOMAS AYRES, 1855

This I shall endeavor to demonstrate in giving the names applied to different localities in the valley and vicinity.

While I was endeavoring to ascertain the names of localities from Ten-ie-ya, he was allowed some privileges in camp, but was not permitted to leave his guard. The cunning old fellow watched his opportunity, and again made an attempt to escape by swimming the river; but he was again foiled, and captured by the watchfulness and surprising strength of Sergeant Cameron.

From this time Ten-ie-ya was secured by a rope which was fastened around his waist. The only liberty allowed was the extent of the rope with which he was fastened. He was a hearty feeder, and was liberally supplied. From a lack of sufficient exercise, his appetite cloyed, and he suffered from indigestion. He made application to Captain Boling for permission to go out from camp to the place where the grass was growing, saying the food he had been supplied with was too strong; that if he did not have grass he should die. He said the grass looked good to him, and there was plenty of it. Why, then, should he not have it, when dogs were allowed to eat it?

The captain was amused at the application, with its irony, but surmised that he was meditating another attempt to leave us; however, he good-humoredly said: "He can have a ton of fodder if he desires it, but I do not think it advisable to turn him loose to graze." The captain consented to the sergeant's kindly arrangements to *tether* him, and he was led out to graze upon the young clover, sorrel, bulbous roots and fresh growth of ferns which were then springing up in the valley, one species of which we found a good salad. All of these he devoured with the relish of a hungry ox. Occasionally truffles or wood-mushrooms were brought him by Sandino and our allies, as if in kindly sympathy for him, or in acknowledgment of his rank. Such presents and a slight deference to his standing as a chief, were always received with grunts of satisfaction. He was easily flattered by any extra attentions to his pleasure. At such times he was singularly amiable and conversational. Like many white men, it was evident that his more liberal feelings could be the easiest aroused through his stomach.

Our supplies not being deemed sufficient for the expedition over the Sierras, and as those verdureless mountains would provide no forage for our animals, nor game to lengthen out our rations unless we descended to the lower levels, Captain Boling sent a pack train to the Fresno for barley and extra rations. All of our Indians except Sandino and Ten-ie-ya were allowed to go below with the detachment sent along as escort for the train. While waiting for these supplies, some of the command who had been exploring up Indian Cañon, reported fresh signs at the head of that ravine. Feeling somewhat recovered in strength, Captain Boling decided to undertake a trip out, and see for himself some of our surroundings. Accordingly, the next morning, he started with some thirty odd men up Indian Cañon. His design was to explore the Scho-look or Scho-tal-lo-wi branch (Yosemite Creek) to its source, or at least the southern exposures of the divide as far east as we could go and return at night. Before starting, I advised the taking of our blankets, for a bivouac upon the ridge, as from experience I was aware of the difficult and laborious ascent, and intimated that the excursion would be a laborious one for an invalid, if the undertaking was accomplished. The captain laughed as he said: "Are your distances equal to your heights? If they correspond, we shall have ample time!" Of course, I could make no reply, for between us, the subject of heights had already been exhausted, although the captain had not yet been to the top of the inclosing walls.

Still, realizing the sensitive condition of his lungs, and his susceptibility to the influences of the cold and light mountain air, I knew it would not be prudent for him to camp at the snow line; and yet I doubted his ability to return the same day; for this reason I felt it my duty to caution him. A few others, who had avoided climbing the cliffs, or if they had been upon any of the high ridges, their mules had taken them there, joined in against my suggestion of providing for the bivouac. I have before referred to the Texan's devotion to the saddle. In it, like Comanche Indians, he will undergo incredible hardships; out of it, he is soon tired, and waddles laboriously like a sailor, until the unaccustomed muscles adapt themselves to the new service required of them; but the probabilities are against the new exercise being continued long enough to accomplish this result. Understanding this, I concluded in a spirit of jocularity to make light of the toil myself; the more so, because I knew that my good captain had no just conception of the labor before him. By a rude process of measurement, and my practical experience in other mountains in climbing peaks whose heights had been established by measurements, I had approximately ascertained or concluded that my first estimate of from fifteen hundred to two thousand feet for the height of El Capitan, was much below the reality. I had so declared in discussing these matters. Captain Boling had finally estimated the height not to exceed one thousand feet. Doctor Black's estimate was far below this. I therefore felt assured that *a walk up* the cañon would practically improve their judgments of height and distance, and laughed within myself in anticipation of the fun in store. On starting, I was directed to take charge of Ten-ie-ya, whom we were to take with us, and to keep Sandino near me, to interpret anything required during the trip. As we entered Indian Cañon, the old chief told the captain that the ravine was a bad one to ascend. To this the captain replied, "No matter, we know this ravine leads out of the valley; Ten-ie-ya's trail might lead us to a warmer locality."

Climbing over the wet, mossy rocks, we reached a level where a halt was called for a rest. As Doctor Black came up from the rear, he pointed to a ridge above us, and exclaimed, "Thank God, we are in sight of the top at last." "Yes, doctor," said I, "that is one of the first tops." "How so?" he inquired; "is not that the summit of this ravine?" To this I cheerfully replied, "You will find quite a number of such tops before you emerge from this cañon." Noticing his absence before reaching the summit, I learned he took the trail back, and safely found his weary way to camp. Captain Boling had overestimated his strength and endurance. He was barely able to reach the table-land at the head of the ravine, where, after resting and lunching, he visited the Falls, as he afterwards informed me. By his order I took command of nine picked men and the two Indians. With these I continued the exploration, while the party with the captain *explored* the vicinity of the High Fall, viewed the distant mountains, and awaited my return from above.

With my energetic little squad, I led the way, old Ten-ie-ya in front, Sandino at his side, through forest openings and meadows, until we reached the open rocky ground on the ridge leading to what is now known as Mt. Hoffman. I directed our course towards that peak. We had not traveled very far, the distance does not now impress me, when as we descended toward a tributary of Yosemite Creek, we came suddenly upon an Indian, who at the moment of discovery was lying down drinking from the brook. The babbling waters had prevented his hearing our approach. We hurried up to within fifty or sixty yards, hoping to capture him, but were discovered. Seeing his supposed danger, he bounded off, a fine specimen of youthful vigor. No race-horse or greyhound could have seemingly made better time than he towards a dense forest in the valley of the Scho-look. Several rifles were raised, but I gave the order "don't shoot," and compelled the old chief to call to him to stop. The young Indian did stop, but it was at a safe distance. When an attempt was made by two or three to move ahead and get close to him, he saw the purpose and again started; neither threatening rifles, nor the calls of Ten-ie-ya could again stop his flight.

As we knew our strength, after such a climb, was not equal to the chase of the fleet youth, he was allowed to go unmolested. I could get no information from Ten-ie-ya concerning the object of the exploration; and as for San-dino, his memory seemed to have conveniently failed him. With this conclusion I decided to continue my course, and moved off rapidly. Ten-ie-ya complained of fatigue, and Sandino reminded me that I was traveling very fast. My reply to both cut short all attempts to lessen our speed; and when either were disposed to lag in their gait, I would cry out the Indian word, "We-teach," meaning hurry up, with such emphasis as to put new life into their movements.

We soon struck an old trail that led east along the south-ern slope of the divide, and when I abandoned my purpose of going farther towards the Tuolumne, and turned to the right on the trail discovered, Ten-ie-ya once more found voice in an attempt to dissuade me from this purpose, say-ing that the trail led into the mountains where it was very cold, and where, without warm clothing at night, we would freeze. He was entirely too earnest, in view of his previous taciturnity; and I told him so.

The snow was still quite deep on the elevated portions of the ridge and in shaded localities, but upon the open ground, the trail was generally quite bare. As we reached a point still farther east, we perceived the trail had been recently used; the tracks had been made within a day or two. From the appearances, we concluded they were made by Ten-ie-ya's scouts who had followed down the ridge and slope west of the North Dome to watch our movements. The tracks were made going and returning, thus showing a continued use of this locality. As the tracks diverged from the trail at this point, they led out of the direct line of any communication with the valley, and after some reflection, I was satisfied that we had struck a clue to their hiding-place, and realizing that it was time to return if we expected to reach the valley before dark, we turned about and started at once on the down grade.

We found the captain anxiously awaiting our return. He was pleased with our report, and agreed in the conclusion that the Indians were encamped not very far off. Captain Boling had suffered from fatigue and the chill air of the mountains. In speaking of a farther pursuit of our discoveries, he said: "I am not as strong as I supposed, and will have to await the return of the pack train before taking part in these expeditions."

I told Captain Boling that upon the trip, Sandino had appeared willfully ignorant when questioned concerning the country we were exploring, and my belief that he stood in fear of Ten-ie-ya; that as a guide, no dependence could be placed upon him, and that his interpretations of Ten-ie-ya's sayings were to be received with caution when given in the old chief's presence, as Ten-ie-ya's Spanish was about equal to his own. Captain Boling instructed me to tell Sandino, that in future, he need only act as interpreter. He seemed satisfied with this arrangement, and said that the country appeared different from what it was when he was a boy and had been accustomed to traverse it.

When we commenced our descent into the valley Ten-ie-ya wanted us to branch off to the left, saying he was very tired, and wanted to take the best trail. Said he, "There is a good trail through the arrow-wood rocks to the left of the cañon." I reported this to the captain, and expressed the opinion that the old chief was sincere for once; he had grumbled frequently while we were ascending the cañon in the morning, because we were compelled to climb over the moss-covered boulders, while crossing and re-crossing the stream, and he told Sandino that we should have taken the trail along the cliff above. Captain Boling replied: "Take it, or it will be long after dark before we reach camp." Accordingly I let Ten-ie-ya lead the way, and told him to travel fast. He had more than once proved that he possessed an agility beyond his years. As his parole was at a discount, I secured a small cord about his chest and attached the other end to my left wrist to maintain *telegraphic* communication with him; but as the hidden trail narrowed and wound its crooked way around a jutting point of the cliff overlooking the valley and ravine, I slipped the loop from my wrist and ordered a halt.

Captain Boling and the men with him came up and took in the view before us. One asked if I thought a bird could go down there safely. Another wanted to know if I was aiding "Old Truthful" to commit suicide. The last question had an echo of suspicion in my own thoughts. I immediately surmised it possible the old sachem was leading us into another trap, where, by some preconcerted signal, an avalanche of rocks would precipitate us all to the bottom. I asked Ten-ie-ya if this trail was used by his people; he assured me it was, by women and children; that it was a favorite trail of his. Seeing some evidences of it having been recently used, and being assured by Sandino that it was somewhere below on this trail that Ten-ie-ya had descended to the valley when taken a prisoner, a few of us were shamed into a determination to make the attempt to go where the old chief could go.

Most of the party turned back. They expressed a willingness to fight Indians, but they had not, they said, the faith requisite to attempt to walk on water, much less air. They went down Indian Cañon, and some did not reach camp until after midnight, tired, bruised and footsore. We who had decided to take our chances, re-commenced our descent. I told Ten-ie-ya to lead on, and to stop at the word "halt," or he would be shot. I then dispatched Sandino across the narrow foot-way, which, at this point was but a few inches in width, and which was all there was dividing us from Eternity as we passed over it. Telling them both to halt on a projecting bench in view, I crossed this yawning abyss, while Sandino, aided by a very dead shot above, held the old man as if petrified, until I was able once more to resume my charge of him.

This I found was the only really dangerous place, on what was facetiously called, by those who were leaving us, "a very good trail." The last fifty or sixty feet of the descent was down the sloping side of an immense detached rock, and then down through the top of a black oak tree at the southwesterly base of the vast cliff or promontory known as the "Arrow-wood Cliff." The "Royal Arches," the "Washington Column" and the "North Dome" occupy positions east of this trail, but upon the same vast pile of granite.

I sometime afterward pointed out the trail to a few visitors that I happened to meet at its foot. They looked upon me with an incredulous leer, and tapped their foreheads significantly, muttering something about "Stockton Asylum." Fearing to trust my amiability too far, I turned and left them. Since then I have remained cautiously silent. Now that the impetuosity of youth has given place to the more deliberate counsels of age, and all dangers to myself or others are past, I repeat, for the benefit of adventurous tourists, that on the southwesterly face of the cliff overlooking the valley and Indian Cañon, there is a trail hidden from view, that they may travel if they will, and experience all the sensations that could ever have been felt, while alive, by a Blondin or LaMountain.

This portion of the cliff we designated as Ten-ie-ya's Trail.

The names of the different objects and localities of especial interest have now become well established by use. It is not a matter of so much surprise that there is such a difference in the orthography of the names. I only wonder that they have been retained in a condition to be recognized. It is not altogether the fault of the interpreters that discrepancies exist in interpretation or pronunciation, although both are often undesignedly warped to conform to the ideality of the interpreter. Many of the names have been modernized and adorned with *transparencies* in order to illuminate the subject of which the parties were writing. Those who once inhabited this region, and gave distinctive appellations, have all disappeared. The names given by them can be but indifferently preserved or counterfeited by their camp followers, the "California Diggers;" but June* is now with us, and we must hasten on to our work of following up the trail.

---

*Perhaps it was late May. See footnote on page 159.

CAPTURING THE YOSEMITES AT LAKE TENAYA

A MOUNTAIN storm raged with such violence as to stampede the mules of the pack-train while the escort were encamped on the South Fork. The mules were not overtaken until they reached the foothills of the Fresno. In the meantime, while impatiently awaiting their return, our rations gave out. In order to somewhat appease our hunger, Dr. Black distributed his hospital stores among us. There were some canned fruits and meats, and several cans of oysters and clams. The southerners of the command waived their rights to the clams, but cast lots for the oysters. Thinking we had a prize in the clams, we brought to bear our early recollections of eastern life, and compounded a most excellent and, what we supposed would be, a most nourishing soup. Our enjoyment, however, of this highly prized New England dish was of short duration; for from some cause, never satisfactorily explained by Dr. Black, *or other eminent counsel,* our eastern mess, as if moved by one impulse of re-gurgitation, *gave up their clams.* Fortunately for us our supplies arrived the next morning; for the game procurable was not sufficient for the command. Major Savage sent Cow-chitty, a brother of Pon-watch-ee, the chief of the Noot-choo band, whose village we surprised before we discovered the valley, as chief of scouts. He was accompanied by several young warriors, selected because they were all familiar with the Sierra Nevada trails and the territory of the Pai-utes, where it was thought probable the expedition would penetrate.

Captain Boling had in his report to Major Savage, complained of the incapacity of Sandino as guide, and expressed the opinion that he stood in awe of Ten-ie-ya. By letter, the major replied, and particularly advised Captain Boling that implicit confidence could be placed in Cow-chitty and his scouts, as the sub-chief was an old enemy of Ten-ie-ya, and was esteemed for his sagacity and woodcraft, which was superior to that of any Indian in his tribe. Captain Boling had improved in health and strength, and concluded to venture on his contemplated expedition over the mountains. He at once ordered preparations to be made. A camp guard was detailed, and a special supply train fitted out. All was ready for a start in the morning. During the evening Captain Boling consulted our new guide as to what trail would be best to follow to the Mono Pass and over the mountains. Cow-chitty had already learned from our Po-ho-no scouts and those of his own tribe, the extent of our explorations, and had had a long talk with Sandino as well as with Ten-ie-ya. The Mission Indian and the old chief tried to make the new guide believe that the Yosemites had gone over the mountains to the Monos. Indian-like, he had remained very grave and taciturn, while the preparations were going on for the expedition. Now, however, that he was consulted by Captain Boling, he was willing enough to give his advice, and in a very emphatic manner declared his belief to the captain that Ten-ie-ya's people were not far off; that they were either hiding in some of the rocky cañons in the vicinity of the valley, or in those of the Tuolumne, and discouraged the idea of attempting the expedition with horses. Although this did not coincide with the views of our captain, the earnestness of Cow-chitty decided him to make another attempt in the near vicinity before crossing the mountains. The horses and supply train were accordingly left in camp, and we started at daylight on foot, with three days' rations packed in our blankets. We left the valley this time by way of the Py-we-ack Cañon, and ascended the north cliff trail, a short distance above "Mirror Lake." Soon after reaching the summit, Indian signs were discovered near the trail we were on. The old trail up the slope of the cañon was here abandoned and the fresh trail followed up to and along the ridges just below the snow line. These signs and the tortuous course pursued were similar to the tracks followed on our trip up Indian Cañon, and were as easily traced until we reached an elevation almost entirely covered with snow from five to ten feet deep, except on exposed tops of ridges, where the snow had blown off to the north side or melted away.

I had accompanied our guide in advance of the command, but observing that our course was a zig-zag one, sometimes almost doubling on our trail, I stopped and told the guide to halt until the captain came up. He had been following the ridges without a sign of a trail being visible, although he had sometimes pointed to small pieces of coarse granite on the rocky divides, which he said had been displaced by Ten-ie-ya's scouts; that in going out or returning from their camps, they had kept on the rocky ridges, and had avoided tracking the snow or soft ground, so as to prevent the Americans from following them. As we stopped, he called me a little out of hearing of those with me, and by pantomime and a few words indicated his belief in the near presence of Indians.

When the captain came up he said: "The hiding-place of the Yosemites is not far off. If they had crossed the mountains their scouts would not be so careful to hide their trail. They would follow the old trail if they came to watch you, because it is direct, and would only hide their tracks when they were again far from the valley and near their rancheria.'' This was, in part, an answer to Captain Boling's inquiry as to why we had left the old trail, and gone so far out of our way. I explained to him what Cow-chitty had stated, and pointed out what the guide or scout said was a fresh trail. The captain looked tired and dis-heartened, but with a grim smile said: ''That may be a fresh Indian track, but I can't see it. If left to my own feelings and judgment, I should say we were on another wild-goose chase. If the guide can see tracks, and thinks he has got 'em this time, I reckon it is better to follow on; but if there is any short-cut tell him to give us some land-marks to go by; for I find I am not as strong as I thought. Let us take another look at this *fresh* trail, and then you may get Cow-chitty's idea as to the probable course this trail will take further on.'' As we moved up the trail a little farther, the expert scout pointed out more fresh signs, but Captain Boling failed to discern a trail, and gave up the examination, and as he seated himself for a momen-tary rest, said: ''I reckon it is all right, Doc. The major says in his letter that I can bet on Cow-chitty every time. But I can't see any more of a trail on this rocky ridge than I can see the trail of that wood-pecker as he flies through the air, but I have some faith in instinct, for I reckon that is what it is that enables him to follow a trail that he imagines should be there. We shall have to trust him to follow it, and let him have his own way as you would a fox-hound; if he don't, puppy-like, take the back track, or run wild with us over some of these ledges.'' Old Ten-ie-ya was now appealed to for information concerning the fresh signs, but he only reiterated his former statement that his people had gone over the mountains to the Monos, and the signs he said were those of Tuolumne Indians. Captain Boling had taken the old chief along with us on this trip, hoping to make him of some use, if not directly as guide, indirectly; it was thought he might betray his people's hiding-place. But the captain was disappointed in this, for no finished gamester ever displayed a more immovable countenance than did Ten-ie-ya when questioned at any time during the expedition. A cord had again been placed around his waist to secure his allegiance, and as we were about to move ahead once more, he very gravely said that if we followed the signs, they would take us over to the Tuolumne.

Before this Sandino had professed to agree with Ten-ie-ya, but now he carefully withheld his own opinions, and as carefully rendered his interpretations. He feared Cow-chitty more than Ten-ie-ya; and he was frequently seen to cross himself while muttering his prayers. Spencer and myself reassured the timid creature, and made him quite happy by telling him that we would guard him against the "Gentiles," as he called the natives.

I explained to Cow-chitty our inability to follow the tracks as he did over the bare granite. This flattered him, and he then pointed out his own method of doing so, which was simple enough with one of keen sight. It consisted entirely in discovering fragments of stone and moss that had been displaced, and broken off and scattered upon the ground. The upper surface of the broken fragments of stone were smooth and bleached, while the under surface was dark or colored. It was impossible to walk over these stony ridges without displacing some of the fragments, and these the quick eye of Cow-chitty was sure to discover. Cow-chitty was pleased when told of Captain Boling's appreciation of his sagacity, and honored by the confidence the captain began to show him. He expressed his gratification by being more communicative than he had been before. He said: "These signs tell me that the Yosemite scouts have been watching all the movements of the Americans, and the trails that will take you to their camps. They will not look for you on this trail. They are watching for you from the ridges nearer the valley. We will not have to go far to find their camps. This trail will lead us to the head of the Py-we-ack, where the Pai-ute or Mono trail crosses into the upper valley of the Tuolumne; and if we don't find them at the lake, we will soon know if they have crossed the mountains."

He then proposed that Captain Boling send out scouts to intercept and capture the Yosemite scouts, who might be below us watching the valley. This being interpreted to Captain Boling, he at once adopted the suggestion of the scout. He selected three of our best runners, and directed Cow-chitty to select three of his. These were sent out in pairs—an Indian and a white man. The scouts were placed under direction of the sub-chief, who followed the trail, and indicated to the captain the most direct route for the main body to follow. In health Captain Boling was athletic and ambitious on the march. He had now, however, overestimated his strength, and suffered considerably from fatigue; but the halt afforded him a rest that very much refreshed him. I traveled with him during the remainder of the march, so as to be near him as interpreter, and took charge of Ten-ie-ya. The captain, Ten-ie-ya, Sandino and myself traveled together. Our march was more leisurely than in the earlier part of the day. This allowed Captain Boling to somewhat recover from his fatigue.

On an ascending spur that ran down to the Py-we-ack, we found Cow-chitty quietly awaiting our approach. As we halted, he pointed out to Captain Boling a dim circle of blue smoke, that appeared to eddy under the lee of a large granite knob or peak, and said, "Rancheria." Old Ten-ie-ya was standing in front of me, but exhibited no interest in the discovery. As I lowered my line of vision to the base of the cliff, to trace the source of the smoke, there appeared the Indian village, resting in fancied security, upon the border of a most beautiful little lake, seemingly not more than a half mile away. To the lake I afterwards gave the name of Ten-ie-ya. The granite knob was so bare, smooth and glistening, that Captain Boling at once pointed it out, and selected it as a landmark. He designated it as a rallying point for his men, if scattered in pursuit, and said that we should probably camp near it for the night.

While the captain was studying the nature of the ground before us, and making his arrangements to capture the village, our scouts were discovered in full chase of an Indian picket, who was running towards the village as if his life depended upon his efforts. In the excitement of the moment Captain Boling ordered us to double-quick and charge, thinking, as he afterwards said, that the huts could not be much more than half a mile away. Such a mistake could only originate in the transparent air of the mountains. The village was fully two miles or more away. We did, however, double-quick, and I kept a gait that soon carried Ten-ie-ya and Sandino, with myself, ahead of our scattering column. Finding the rope with which I held Ten-ie-ya an encumbrance in our rapid march, I wound it round his shoulder and kept him in front of me. While passing a steep slope of overlapping granite rock, the old chief made a sudden spring to the right, and attempted to escape down the ragged precipice. His age was against him, for I caught him just as he was about to let himself drop from the projecting ledge to the ground below; his feet were already over the brink.

I felt somewhat angered at the trick of the old fellow in attempting to relieve himself from my custody, and the delay it had occasioned me; for we had taken the most direct although not the smoothest course. I resumed our advance at a gait that hurried the old sachem forward, perhaps less carefully and more rapidly than comported with the dignity of his years and rank. I was amused at the proposition of one of the "boys" who had witnessed the transaction, to "shoot the old devil, and not be bothered with him any more." I, of course, declined this humane proposition to relieve me of further care, and at once became the chief's most devoted defender, which observing, he afterwards told Captain Boling that I was "very good." As we reached the more gently descending ground near the bottom of the slope, an Indian came running up the trail below us that led to the Rancheria. His course was at an acute angle to the one pursued by us toward the village, which was now but a few rods off. I ordered Sandino to cut him off and capture him before he should reach the camp. This was accomplished with great energy and a good degree of pride.

The Yosemites had already discovered our approach, but too late for any concerted resistance or for successful escape, for Lieutenant Crawford at the head of a portion of the command, dashed at once into the center of the encampment, and the terror-stricken Indians immediately threw up their bare hands in token of submission, and piteously cried out "pace! pace!" (peace, peace). As I halted to disarm the scout captured by Sandino, I was near enough to the camp to hear the expressions of submission. I was compelled to laugh at the absurd performances of Sandino, who to terrify his prisoner, was persistently holding in his face an old double-barreled pistol. I was aware the weapon was a harmless one, for one hammer was gone, and the other could not be made to explode a cap. I took the bow and arrows from the frightened savage, and as Captain Boling came up I reported the capture, telling him at the same time of the surrender of the village or Rancheria to Lieutenant Crawford. Seeing some of the Indians leaving the camp, and running down the lake to a trail crossing its outlet, the captain and the men with him sprang forward through the grove of pines near the crossing, and drove them back. No show of resistance was offered, neither did any escape from us.

While Captain Boling was counting his prisoners and corralling them with a guard, I, by his previous order, restrained Ten-ie-ya from any communication with his people. The chief of this village was a young man of perhaps thirty years of age. When called upon by the captain to state how many were under his command, he answered that those in the encampment were all that was left; the rest had scattered and returned to the tribes they sprung from. Ten-ie-ya seemed very anxious to answer the interrogations made to the young chief, but Captain Boling would not allow his further interference, and jokingly told me to send him over among the women who were grouped a little aside, as he was now about as harmless. I acted upon the suggestion, and upon his being told that he had the liberty of the camp if he made no further attempts to escape, the old fellow stepped off briskly to meet his four squaws, who were with this band, and who seemed as pleased as himself at their reunion.

Captain Boling felt satisfied that the answer given by this half-starved chief, and the few braves of his wretched-looking band, were as truthful as their condition would corroborate. Finding themselves so completely surprised, notwithstanding their extreme vigilance, and comparing the well-kept appearance of their old chief with their own worn-out, dilapidated condition, they with apparent anxiety expressed a willingness for the future to live in peace with the Americans. All hopes of avoiding a treaty, or of preventing their removal to the Reservation, appeared to have at once been abandoned; for when the young chief was asked if he and his band were willing to go to the Fresno, he replied with much emotion of gesture, and as rendered by Sandino to Spencer and myself: "Not only willing, but anxious;" for, said he: "Where can we now go that the Americans will not follow us?" As he said this, he stretched his arms out toward the East, and added: "Where can we make our homes, that you will not find us?" He then went on and stated that they had fled to the mountains without food or clothing; that they were worn out from watching our scouts, and building *signal-fires* to tire us out also.

They had been anxious to embroil us in trouble by drawing us into the cañons of the Tuolumne, where were some Pai-utes wintering in a valley like Ah-wah-ne. They had hoped to be secure in this retreat until the snow melted, so that they could go to the Mono tribe and make a home with them, but that now he was told the Americans would follow them even there, he was willing, with all his little band, to go to the plains with us. After the young chief had been allowed full liberty of speech, and had sat down, Ten-ie-ya again came forward, and would have doubtless made a *confession of faith*, but his speech was cut short by an order from Captain Boling to at once move camp to a beautiful pine grove on the north side of the outlet to the lake, which he had selected for our camping-place for the night. By this order he was able to have everything in readiness for an early start the next morning. There was an abundance of dry pine, convenient for our camp-fires, and as the night

*Probably Hetch Hetchy Valley

was exceedingly cold, the glowing fires were a necessity to our comfort. The Indians were told to pack such movables as they desired to take with them, and move down at once to our camp-ground.

The scene was a busy one. The squaws and children exhibited their delight in the prospect of a change to a more genial locality, and where food would be plenty. While watching the preparations of the squaws for the transfer of their household treasures and scanty stores, my attention was directed to a dark object that appeared to be crawling up the base of the first granite peak above their camp. The polished surface of the gleaming rock made the object appear larger than the reality. We were unable to determine what kind of an animal it could be; but one of our scouts, to whom the name of "Big Drunk" had been given, pronounced it a papoose, although some had variously called it a bear, a fisher or a coon. "Big Drunk" started after it and soon returned with a bright, active boy, entirely naked, which he coaxed from his slippery perch. Finding himself an object of curiosity his fright subsided, and he drew from its hiding-place, in the bushes near by, a garment that somewhat in shape, at least, resembled a man's shirt. *"The Glistening Rocks"* had rendered us all oblivious to the color, and that was left undetermined. This garment swept the ground after he had clothed himself with it. His ludicrous appearance excited our laughter, and as if pleased with the attentions paid to him, the little fellow joined heartily in the merriment he occasioned. It will not be out of place to here relate the sequel of this boy's history. Learning that he was an orphan and without relatives, Captain Boling adopted him, calling him "Reube," in honor of Lieutenant Reuben Chandler, who after Captain Boling was the most popular man in the battalion. Some three or four years afterward, the boy, as if to illustrate the folly of the captain in trying to civilize and educate him, ran away from his patron, taking with him two valuable, thoroughbred Tennessee horses, much prized by the captain; besides money, clothing and arms belonging to the captain's brother-in-law, Colonel Lane of Stockton, in whose charge Captain Boling had placed him, that he might have the advantages of a good school.

After collecting together all the Indians found in this encampment, the total number was found to be but thirty-five, nearly all of whom were in some way a part of the family of the old patriarch, Ten-ie-ya. These were escorted to our camp, the men placed under guard, but the women and children were left free.

This was accomplished before sundown, and being relieved of duty, a few of us ran across the outlet of the lake, and climbing the divide on the south side of the lake, beheld a sunset view that will long be remembered. It was dark when we reached camp, and after a scanty repast, we spread our blankets, and soon were wrapped in slumber sweet.

We were awakened by the cold, which became more uncomfortable as night advanced, and finding it impossible to again compose ourselves to sleep, Captain Boling aroused the camp, and preparations were made by the light of the blazing camp-fires for an early start for the valley. Desiring some clean, fresh water, I went to the lake as the nearest point to obtain it, when, to my surprise, I found that the new ice formed during the night and connecting the old ice with the shore of the lake, was strong enough to bear me up. At a point where the old ice had drifted near, I went out some distance upon it, and it appeared strong enough to have borne up a horse. This was about the 5th of June, 1851.* The change of temperature from summer in the valley to winter on the mountains, without shelter, was felt by us all. After a hasty breakfast, the word was passed to

*reported as May 23, 1851, by Carl P. Russell in *100 Years in Yosemite*, 1957, p. 39.

assemble, and we were soon all ready for the order to march. All at once there was turmoil and strife in camp, and what sounded to my ears very much like a Chinese concert. Captain Boling was always a man of gallantry, and in this instance would not allow the squaws to take the burden of the baggage. Hence the confusion and delay. He ordered the Indians to carry the packs—burdens they had imposed on their women. This order brought down upon him the vituperations of the squaws and sullen murmurs from the "noble red men;" as often happens in domestic interference, *the family was offended*. Ten-ie-ya rose to explain, and waxed eloquent in his protest against this innovation on their ancient customs.

As soon as the captain was made aware of the old fellow's object in having "a talk," he cut short the debate by ordering one of the lieutenants to see that every Indian, as well as squaw, was properly loaded with a just proportion of their burdens. The real object of the captain was to facilitate the return to the valley, by making it easy for the squaws and children to accompany us through without delays. One amusing feature in this arrangement was, that long after the men had been silenced, their squaws continued to murmur at the indignity practiced on their disgraced lords. I have my doubts, even to this day, whether the standard of women's rights was ever again *waved* among the mountain tribes after this "special order" was issued by our good-hearted captain.

In order to take the most direct route to the valley, Captain Boling selected one of the young Yosemite Indians to lead the way with our regular guide. Being relieved of the charge of Ten-ie-ya, I took my usual place on the march with the guide. This position was preferred by me, because it afforded ample opportunity for observation and time for reflection; and beside, it was in my nature to be in advance. The trail followed, after leaving the lake, led us over bare granite slopes and hidden paths, but the distance was mate- rially shortened. A short distance below the bottom land of the lake, on the north side of the cañon and at the head of the gorge, the smooth, sloping granite projects like a vast roof over the abyss below. As we approached this, our young guide pointed toward it.

By close observation I was able to discover that the trail led up its sloping surface, and was assured by the guide that the trail was a good one. I felt doubtful of the cap- tain's willingness to scale that rocky slope, and halted for him to come up. The captain followed the trail to its ter- mination in the soil, and saw the cause of my having halted. Upon the discoloration of the rock being pointed out as the continuation of the trail, he glanced up the granite slope and said, "Go on, but be watchful, for a slide into the gorge would bring as certain death as a slide from that San Joaquin trail, which I have not yet forgotten." Some of the command did not fancy this any more than they did the Ten-ie-ya trail down "Indian Cañon." We all pulled off our boots and went up this slope barefooted. Seeing there was no real danger, the most timid soon moved up as fear- less as the others. I, with the advance, soon reached the soil above, and at the top halted until the Indians and our straggling column closed up. As I looked about me, I dis- covered, unfolding to my sight, one of the most charming views in this sublimest scenery of nature.* During the day before, we had looked with astonishment on the almost boundless peaks, and snow-capped mountains, to be seen from the Mt. Hoffman divide. But here some of the same views appeared illuminated. In our ascent up the moun- tain, we had apparently met the rising sun. The scene was one long to be remembered for its brilliancy, although not describable.

*They were near, if not at, Olmsted Point on today's Tioga Road.

Mr. Addison, in the *Spectator,* says: "Our imagination loves to be filled with an object, or to grasp at anything that is too big for its capacity. We are flung into a pleasing astonishment at such unbounded views, and feel a delightful stillness and amazement in the soul." Mr. Addison has here expressed the feelings entertained by some of us, as the view met our gaze while looking out to the east, the south and the west. Although not sufficiently elevated to command a general outlook, the higher ridges framing some of the scenery to the north and eastward of us, the westerly view was boundless. The transparency of the atmosphere was here extreme, and as the sun illumined the snow-clad and ice-burnished peaks, the scene aroused the enthusiasm of the command to a shout of glad surprise.

The recollections of the discomforts of the night were banished by the glory of the morning as here displayed. Even the beauties of the Yosemite, of which I was so ardent an admirer, were for the moment eclipsed by this gorgeously grand and changing scene. The aurora that had preceded the rising sun was as many-hued, and if possible more glorious, than the most vivid borealis of the northern climes. But when the sun appeared, seemingly like a sudden flash, amidst the distant peaks, the climax was complete. My opportunities for examining the mountain scenery of the Sierra Nevada above the immediate vicinity of the Yosemite, were such as to only enable me to give a somewhat general description, but the views that I had during our explorations afforded me glimpses of the possibilities of sublime mountain scenery, such as I had never before comprehended, although familiar with the views afforded from some of the peaks of Mexico and of the Rocky Mountains. I doubt even if the Yellowstone, supreme in some of its attractions, affords such varied and majestic beauty.

Looking back to the lovely little lake, where we had been encamped during the night, and watching Ten-ie-ya as he ascended to our group, I suggested to the captain that we name the lake after the old chief, and call it "Lake Ten-ie-ya." The captain had fully recovered from his annoyance at the scene in camp, and readily consented to the name, but added that I had evidently mistaken my vocation.

Noticing my look of surprise, he jokingly said that if I had only studied divinity instead of medicine, I could have then fully gratified my passion for christening. This, of course, brought out a general guffaw, and thinking me annoyed, he said: "Gentlemen, I think the name an appropriate one, and shall use it in my report of the expedition. Beside this, it is rendering a kind of justice to perpetuate the name of the old chief."

When Ten-ie-ya reached the summit, he left his people and approached where the captain and a few of us were halting. Although he had been snubbed by the captain that morning, he now seemed to have forgotten it, and his rather rugged countenance glowed with healthful exercise in the sunlight. I had handled him rather roughly the day before, but as he now evidently wished to be friendly, I called him up to us, and told him that we had given his name to the lake and river. At first, he seemed unable to comprehend our purpose, and pointing to the group of Glistening peaks, near the head of the lake, said: "It already has a name; we call it Py-we-ack."* Upon my telling him that we had named it Ten-ie-ya, because it was upon the shores of the lake that we had found his people, who would never return to it to live, his countenance fell and he at once left our group and joined his own family circle. His countenance as he left us indicated that he thought the naming of the lake no equivalent for the loss of his territory.

*translated as "Lake of the Glistening Rocks"

I never at any time had real personal dislike for the old sachem. He had always been an object of study, and I sometimes found in him profitable entertainment. As he moved off to hide his sorrow, I pitied him. As we resumed our march over the rough and billowy trail, I was more fully impressed with the appropriateness of the name for the beautiful lake. Here, probably, his people had built their last wigwams in their mountain home. From this lake we were leading the last remnant of his once dreaded tribe, to a territory from which it was designed they should never return as a people. My sympathies, confirmed in my own mind, a justness in thus perpetuating the name of Ten-ie-ya. The Indian name for this lake, branch and cañon, "Py-we-ack" is, although a most appropriate one, now displaced by that of the old chief Ten-ie-ya. Of the signification of the name Ten-ie-ya, I am uncertain; but as pronounced by himself, I have no doubt of its being pure Indian.

LAKE TENAYA, ONE OF THE YOSEMITE FOUNTAINS.

We reached our camp in the valley without accident. Captain Boling at once gave orders to make preparations for our return to the Fresno. The next day we broke camp and moved down to the lower end of the valley near where we camped on the first night of our discovery, near the little meadow at the foot of the Mariposa Trail.

At sunrise the next morning, or rather as the reflections on the cliffs indicated sunrise, we commenced our ascent of the steep trail. As I reached the height of land where the moving column would soon perhaps forever shut out from view the immortal "Rock Chief," my old sympathies returned, and leaving the command to pursue its heedless way, I climbed to my old perch where Savage had warned me of danger. As I looked back upon El Capitan, his bald forehead was cooling in the breeze that swept by me from the *"Summer land" below*, and his cheerful countenance reflected back the glory of the rising sun. Feeling my own inferiority while acknowledging the majesty of the scene, I looked back from Mt. Beatitude, and quoting from Bacon, exclaimed:

> Yosemite!
> "Thy vale(s) of evergreen, thy hills of snow
> Proclaim thee Nature's varied favorite now."

We reached the Fresno without the loss of a captive, and as we turned them over to the agent, we were formally commended for the success of the expedition.

THE END: OF THE YOSEMITES,
CHIEF TENAYA, AND MAJOR SAVAGE

On arriving at headquarters on the Fresno, with the remnant of the once numerous and defiant band of Yosemite Indians, whose thieving propensities and murderous attacks had made them a dread to miners and "ranche" men, we found a general feeling of confidence that the "Indian war" was ended.

The major at once reported the condition of affairs to the governor, and recommended that the "Mariposa Battalion" be mustered out and honorably discharged from further service.

With many others, I had joined in the operations against the Indians from conscientious motives and in good faith to chastise them for the numerous murders and frequent robberies they were committing. Our object was to compel them to keep the peace, that we might be permitted to live undisturbed by their depredations. We had sufficient general intelligence and knowledge of their character to know that we were looked upon as trespassers on their territory, but were unwilling to abandon our search for gold, or submit to their frequent demands for an ever-increasing tribute. Beside other property, I had lost four valuable horses, which were taken to satisfy their appetites. Neither Bonner's nor Vanderbilt's love for horses, was ever greater than was that of those mountain Indians. No horse was considered too valuable for them to eat. Nothwithstanding all this sense of injury done to my personal interests, I could not justify myself in joining any scheme to wrong them, or rather, the government; and it was too plainly evident that no damages could be obtained for losses, except through the California Indian Ring that was now pretty well established. During the operations of the Bat-

talion, the plans of the Ring were laid, and it was determined that when the war should be ended, "a vigorous
peace policy" should be inaugurated. Estimates of the
probable number of Indians that it would be necessary to
provide for in Mariposa county alone, accidentally fell under my observation, and I at once saw that it was the
design to deceive the government and the people in regard
to the actual number, in order to obtain from Congress
large appropriations. These estimates were cited as official by Col. McKee, and were ten times more than the truth
would warrant. Major Savage justified his course in using
the opportunity to make himself whole again, while acting
as a trader, and in aiding others to secure "a good thing,"
by the sophism that he was not responsible for the action
of the commissioners or of Congress.

AFTER being mustered out, the members of the battalion
at once returned to their various avocations. I was fully
occupied with mining and trading operations, and hence
gave little heed to affairs at the Fresno. Through Captain
Boling, however, who was elected Sheriff of the county,
and whose business carried him to all parts of the country,
I learned of the appointment of Col. Thomas Henly as
agent for the tribes of Mariposa county, and as sub-agents
M. B. Lewis for the Fresno and Wm. J. Campbell for the
King's River Agencies. I afterwards met Col. Henly and
Mr. Lewis in Mariposa, and was much pleased with the
Colonel. Both of these gentlemen were kind and genial;
but Mr. Lewis soon tired of his office as unsuited to his
taste, and accepted a position in the State Government
under Major Roman. His successor, I believe, was Capt.
Vincinthalor. Old Ten-ie-ya, and his band, were never
recipients of friendly favors from Savage, nor was he in
very good standing with the agent. This was known to
the other chiefs, and they frequently taunted him with his

downfall. The old chief chafed under the contemptuous treatment of those who had once feared him and applied to the sub-agent or farmer for permission to go back to his mountain home. He claimed that he could not endure the heat at the agency, and said he preferred acorns to the rations furnished him by the government.

To rid itself of the consequences engendered by these petty squabbles with the old chief, the management at the Fresno consented to a short absence under restrictions. Ten-ie-ya promised to perform all requirements, and joyfully left the hot and dry reservation, and with his family, took the trail to the Yosemite once more. As far as is known, Ten-ie-ya kept faith and disturbed no one. Soon after his departure, however, a few of his old followers quietly left the Fresno as was supposed to join him, but as no complaints were made by their chiefs, it was understood that they were glad to be rid of them; therefore no effort was made to bring them back. During the winter of 1851-52 a considerable number of horses were stolen, but as some of them were found in the possession of Mexicans, who were promptly executed for the theft, no charge was preferred against the Yosemites.

Early in May, 1852, a small party of miners from Coarse Gold Gulch, started out on a prospecting tour with the intention of making a visit to the Yosemite Valley.

The curiosity of some of these men had been excited by descriptions of it, made by some of the ex-members of the Battalion who had gone to Coarse Gold Gulch, soon after their discharge. This party spent some little time prospecting on their way. Commencing on the south fork of the Merced, they tested the mineral resources of streams tributary to it; and then, passing over the divide on the trail, camped for the purpose of testing the branches leading into the main Merced. While at this camp, they were visited by begging Indians; a frequent occurrence in the mining camps of some localities. The Indians appeared friendly, and gave no indications of hostile intentions. They gave the party to understand, however, that the territory they were then in, belonged to them, although no tribute was demanded. The miners comprehended their intimations, but paid no attention to their claim, being aware that this whole region had been ceded to the Government by treaty during the year before.

Having ascertained that they were a part of the Yosemite Band, the miners by signs, interrogated them as to the direction of the valley, but this they refused to answer or pretended not to understand. The valley however, was known to be near, and no difficulty was anticipated, when the party were ready to visit it, as an outline map, furnished them before starting, had thus far proved reliable. Unsuspicious of danger from an attack, they reached the valley, and while entering it on the old trail, were ambushed by the Indians from behind some rocks at or near the foot of the trail, and two of the party were instantly killed. Another was seriously wounded, but finally succeeded in making his escape. The names of the two men killed were Rose and Shurbon; the name of the wounded man was Tudor. *

The reports of these murders, alarmed many of the citizens. They were fearful that the Indians would become excited and leave the reservations, in which case, it was thought, a general outbreak would result. The management of the Fresno agency was censured for allowing Tenie-ya to return to the valley, and for allowing so considerable a number of his followers to again assemble under his leadership. Among the miners, this alarm was soon forgotten, for it was found that instead of leaving the res-

---

*See *100 Years in Yosemite* by Carl P. Russell, page 40, for another version of this episode based on later data in which one of the surviving miners appears to have framed the Indians for his own misdeeds!

ervations, the Indians camped outside, fled to the agencies for protection, lest they should be picked off in revenge for the murders perpetrated by the Yo-sem-i-tes. The officer in command at Fort Miller, was notified of these murders, and a detachment of regular soldiers under Lt. Moore, U. S. A., was at once dispatched to capture or punish the redskins. Beside the detachment of troops, scouts and guides, a few of the friends of the murdered men accompanied the expedition. Among the volunteer scouts, was A. A. Gray, usualy called "Gus" Gray. He had been a member of Captain Boling's company and was with us, when the valley was discovered, as also on our second visit to the valley under Captain Boling. He had been a faithful explorer, and his knowledge of the valley and its vicinity, made his services valuable to Lt. Moore, as special guide and scout for that locality. The particulars of this expedition I obtained from Gray. He was afterward a Captain under Gen. Walker, of Nicaragua notoriety. Under the guidance of Gray, Lt. Moore entered the valley in the night, and was successful in surprising and capturing a party of five savages; but an alarm was given, and Tenie-ya and his people fled from their huts and escaped. On examination of the prisoners in the morning, it was discovered that each of them had some article of clothing that had belonged to the murdered men. The naked bodies of Rose and Shurbon were found and buried. Their graves were * on the edge of the little meadow near the Bridal Veil Fall.

When the captives were accused of the murder of the two white men, they did not deny the charge; but tacitly admitted that they had done it to prevent white men from coming to their valley. They declared that it was their home, and that white men had no right to come there without their consent.

Lieutenant Moore told them, through his interpreter,

*[and still are — ed.]

that they had sold their lands to the Government, that it belonged to the white men now; that the Indians had no right there. They had signed a treaty of peace with the whites, and had agreed to live on the reservations provided for them. To this they replied that Ten-ie-ya had never consented to the sale of their valley and had never received pay for it. The other chiefs, they said, had no right to sell their territory, and no right to laugh at their misfortunes.

Lieutenant Moore became fully satisfied that he had captured the real murderers, and the abstract questions of title and jurisdiction, were not considered debatable in this case. He promptly pronounced judgment, and sentenced them to be shot. They were at once placed in line, and by his order, a volley of musketry from the soldiers announced that the spirits of five Indians were liberated to occupy ethereal space.

This may seem summary justice for a single individual, in a republic, to meet out to fellow beings on his own judgment; but a formal judical killing of these Indians could not have awarded more summary justice. This prompt disposition of the captured murderers, was witnessed by a scout sent out by Ten-ie-ya to watch the movements of Lieutenant Moore and his command, and was immediately reported to the old chief, who with his people at once made a precipitate retreat from their hiding places, and crossed the mountains to their allies, the Pai-utes and Monos. Although this was in June, the snow, which was lighter than the year before at this time, was easily crossed by the Indians and their families. After a short search, in the vicinity of the valley, Lieutenant Moore struck their trail at Lake Ten-ie-ya, and followed them in close pursuit, with an expressed determination to render as impartial justice to the whole band as he had to the five in the valley. It was no disappointment to me to learn from Gray, that when once alarmed, old Ten-ie-ya was too much for Lieutenant Moore, as he had been for Major Savage and Captain Boling. Lieutenant Moore did not overtake the Indians he was pursuing, neither was he able to get any information from the Pai-utes, whom he encountered, while east of the Sierras. Lieutenant Moore crossed the Sierras over the Mono trail that leads by the Soda Springs through the Mono Pass. He made some fair discoveries of gold and gold-bearing quartz, obsidian and other minerals, while exploring the region north and south of Bloody Cañon and of Mono Lake. Finding no traces whatever of the cunning chief, he returned to the Soda Springs, and from there took his homeward journey to Fort Miller by way of the old trail that passed to the south of the Yosemite.

Lieutenant Moore did not discover the Soda Springs nor the Mono Lake country, but he brought into prominent notice the existence of the Yosemite, and of minerals in paying quantities upon the Eastern Slope. Mr. Moore made a brief descriptive report of his expedition, that found its way into the newspapers. At least, I was so informed at the time, though unable to procure it. I saw, however, some severe criticisms of his display of autocratic power in ordering the five Yosemites shot.

PIUTE INDIAN CAPTAIN.

After the establishment of the "Mariposa Chronicle" by W. T. Witachre and A. S. Gould, the first number of which was dated January 20, 1854, Lieutenant Moore, to more fully justify himself or gratify public curiosity, published in the "Chronicle" a letter descriptive of the expedition and its results. In this letter he dropped the terminal letter "y" in the name "Yosemite," as it had been written previously by myself and other members of the battalion, and substituted "e," as before stated. As Lieutenant Moore's article attracted a great deal of public attention at that time, the name, with its present orthography, was accepted.

To Lieutenant Moore belongs the credit of being the first to attract the attention of the scientific and literary world, and "The Press" to the wonders of the Yosemite Valley. His position as an officer of the regular army established a reputation for his article that could not be expected by other correspondents. I was shown by Gray, who was exhibiting them in Mariposa, some very good specimens of gold quartz that were found on the Moore expedition. Leroy Vining and a few chosen companions, with one of Moore's scouts as guide, went over the Sierras to the place where the gold had been found, and established themselves on what has since been known as Vining's Gulch or Creek.*

On the return of Lieutenant Moore to Fort Miller, the news of his capture of the Indians, and his prompt execution of them as the murderers of Rose and Shurbon, occasioned some alarm among the timid, which was encouraged and kept alive by unprincipled and designing politicians. All kinds of vague rumors were put in circulation. Many not in the secret supposed another Indian war would be inaugurated. Political factions and "Indian Rings" encouraged a belief in the most improbable rumors, hoping thereby to influence Congressional action, or operate upon

*Lee Vining today.

the War Department to make large estimates for the California Indian Service.

This excitement did not extend beyond the locality of its origin and the citizens were undisturbed in their industries by these rumors. During all this time no indications of hostilities were exhibited by any of the tribes or bands, although the abusive treatment they received at the hands of some was enough to provoke contention. They quietly remained on the reservations. As far as I was able to learn at the time, a few persons envied them the possession of their King's River reservation, and determined to *"squat"* upon it, after they should have been driven off. This "border element" was made use of by an unprincipled schemer by the name of Harvey, whom it was understood was willing to accept office, when a division of Mariposa county should have been made, or when a vacancy of any kind should occur. But population was required, and the best lands had been reserved for the savages. A few hangers-on, at the agencies, that had been discharged for want of employment and other reasons, made claims upon the King's River reservation; the Indians came to warn them off, when they were at once fired upon, and it was reported that several were killed.

These agitations and murders were denounced by Major Savage in unsparing terms, and he claimed that Harvey was responsible for them. Although the citizens of Mariposa were at the time unable to learn the details of the affair at King's River, which was a distant settlement, the great mass of the people were satisfied that wrong had been done to the Indians. There had been a very decided opposition by the citizens generally to the establishment of two agencies in the county, and the selection of the best agricultural lands for reservations. Mariposa then included nearly the whole San Joaquin Valley south of the Tuolumne.

The opponents to the recommendations of the commissioners claimed that "The government of the United States has no right to select the territory of a sovereign State to establish reservations for the Indians, nor for any other purpose, without the consent of the State." The State Legislature of 1851-52 instructed the Senators and Representatives in Congress to use their influence to have the Indians removed beyond the limits of the State. These views had been advocated by many of the citizens of Mariposa county in good faith; but it was observed that those who most actively annoyed and persecuted those located on King's River reservation were countenanced by those who professed to advocate opposite views. These men were often to be seen at the agency, apparently the welcome guests of the employés of government.

It soon became quite evident that an effort was being made to influence public opinion, and create an impression that there was imminent danger; in order that the general government would thereby be more readily induced to continue large appropriations to keep in subjection the comparatively few savages in the country.

It was a well-known fact that these people preferred horse-flesh and their acorn jelly to the rations of beef that were supposed to have been issued by the government. During this time, Major Savage was successfully pursuing his trade with the miners of the Fresno and surrounding territory, and with the Indians at the agency. Frequently those from the King's River agency would come to Savage to trade, thereby exciting the jealous ire of the King's River traders. Self-interest as well as public good prompted Savage to use every means at his disposal to keep these people quiet, and he denounced Harvey and his associates as entitled to punishment under the laws of the government. These denunciations, of course, reached Harvey and his friends. Harvey and a sub-agent by the name of Campbell seemed most aggrieved at what Savage had said of the affray, and both appeared to make common cause in denouncing the major in return. Harvey made accusations against the integrity of Savage, and boasted that Savage would not dare visit King's River while he, Harvey, was there. As soon as this reached the major's ears, he mounted his horse and at once started for the King's River agency.

Here, as expected, Harvey was found, in good fellowship with Marvin, the quartermaster, and others connected with the agency. Walking up to Harvey, Major Savage demanded of him a retraction of his offensive remarks concerning himself. This Harvey refused to do, and said something to the effect that Savage had talked about Harvey. "Yes," replied Major Savage, "I have said that you are a murderer and a coward." Harvey retreated a pace or two and muttered that it was a lie. As quick as the word was uttered, Savage knocked Harvey down. Harvey appeared to play 'possum and made no resistance. As Savage stooped over the prostrate Harvey, a pistol fell from Savage's waist, seeing which, Marvin picked it up and held it in his hand as the major walked off. Harvey rose to his feet at this moment, and seeing Marvin with the pistol in his hand, exclaimed, "Judge, you have got my pistol!" Marvin replied, "No, I have not. This belongs to Major Savage." When, instantly, Harvey commenced firing at Major Savage, who, though mortally wounded by the first shot, and finding his pistol gone, strove hard to once more reach Harvey, whom he had scorned to further punish when prostrate before him.

This was in August, 1852. Harvey was arrested, or gave himself up, and after the farce of an examination, was discharged. The justice before whom Harvey was examined was a personal friend of the murderer, but had previously fed upon the bounty of Savage. Afterwards, he commenced a series of newspaper articles, assailing the Indian management of California, and these articles culminated in his receiving congenial employment at one of the agencies. Harvey, having killed his man, was now well calculated for a successful California politician of that period, and was triumphantly elected to office; but the ghost of Major Savage seemed to have haunted him, for ever after he was nervous and irritable, and finally died of paralysis. The body of Major Savage was afterwards removed to the Fresno, near his old trading post. A monument was there erected to his memory by Dr. Leach, his successor in business.

During the winter of 1852-3, Jesse Starkey and Mr. Johnson, comrades of the Mariposa Battalion and expert hunters, were engaged in supplying miners along the Mariposa Creek with venison and bear meat. They were encamped on the headwaters of the Chow-chilla and fearing no danger, slept soundly in their encampment. They had met Indians from time to time, who seemed friendly enough, and even the few escaped Yosemites who recognized Starkey, showed no sign of dislike; and hence no proper precautions were taken against their treachery.

A few days only had passed in the occupation of hunting, when a night attack was made upon the hunters. Starkey was instantly killed, but Johnson, though wounded, escaped to Mariposa on one of their mules.

James M. Roan, Deputy Sheriff under Captain Boling, took direction of the wounded man, and with a posse of but fifteen miners, went out to the Chow-chilla, where they found the naked and mutilated remains of poor Starkey, which they buried uncoffined at the camp.

After that sad duty was accomplished, the little party of brave men pursued the trail of the savages into the Snowy Mountains, where they were overtaken and given merited chastisement. Three Indians fell dead at the first fire, while others were wounded and died afterwards.

No united effort was made to repel the whites, and panic-stricken, the renegade robbers fled into their hidden recesses. Cossom, an Indian implicated, confessed, long afterwards, that their loss in the attack was at least a dozen killed and wounded, and that the robber murderers of Starkey were renegade Yosemite and other Indians who had refused to live at the reservation. It was several months after Mr. Roan's encounter with those Indians before I learned the full particulars, and when any of the remnants of the band of Yosemites appealed to me for aid, I still gave them relief.

From these Indians, and subsequently from others, I learned the following statements relative to the death of old Ten-ie-ya. After the murder of the French miners from Coarse Gold Gulch, and his escape from Lieutenant Moore, Ten-ie-ya, with the larger part of his band, fled to the east side of the Sierras. He and his people were kindly received by the Monos and secreted until Moore left that locality and returned to Fort Miller.

Ten-ie-ya was recognized, by the Mono tribe, as one of their number, as he was born and lived among them until his ambition made him a leader and founder of the Pai-ute colony in Ah-wah-ne. His history and warlike exploits formed a part of the traditionary lore of the Monos. They were proud of his successes and boasted of his descent from their tribe, although Ten-ie-ya himself claimed that his father was the chief of an independent people, whose ancestors were of a different race. Ten-ie-ya had, by his cunning and sagacity in managing the deserters from other tribes, who had sought his protection, maintained a reputation as a chief whose leadership was never disputed by his followers, and who was the envy of the leaders of other tribes. After his subjugation by the whites, he was deserted by his followers, and his supremacy was no longer acknowledged by the neighboring tribes, who had feared rather than respected him or the people of his band. Ten-ie-ya and his refugee band were so hospitably received and entertained by the Monos that they seemed in no hurry to return to their valley.

According to custom with these mountaineers, a portion of territory was given to them for their occupancy by consent of the tribe; for individual right to territory is not claimed, nor would it be tolerated. Ten-ie-ya staid with the Monos until late in the summer or early autumn of 1853, when he and his people suddenly left the locality that had been assigned to them, and returned to their haunts in the Yosemite Valley, with the intention of remaining there unless again driven out by the whites. Permanent wigwams were constructed by the squaws, near the head of the valley, among the rocks, not readily discernible to visitors. Not long after Ten-ie-ya had re-established himself in his old home, a party of his young men left on a secret foraging expedition for the camp of the Monos, which was then established at or near Mono Lake. According to the statement made to me, there had just been a successful raid and capture of horses by the Monos and Pai-ute from some of the Southern California ranchos, and Ten-ie-ya's men concluded, rather than risk a raid on the white men, to steal from the Monos, trusting to their cunning to escape detection.

Ten-ie-ya's party succeeded in *recapturing* a few of the stolen horses, and after a circuitous and baffling route through the pass at the head of the San Joaquin, finally reached the valley with their spoils.

After a few days' delay, and thinking themselves secure, they killed one or more of the horses, and were in the enjoyment of a grand feast in honor of their return, when the Monos pounced down upon them. Their gluttony seemed to have rendered them oblivious of all danger to themselves and of the ingratitude by which the feast had been supplied. Like sloths, they appear to have been asleep after having surfeited their appetites. They were surprised in their wigwams by the wronged and vengeful Monos and before they could rally for the fight, the treacherous old chief was struck down by the hand of a powerful young Mono chief. Ten-ie-ya had been the principal object of attack at the commencement of the assault, but he had held the others at bay until discovered by the young chief, who having exhausted his supply of arrows, seized a fragment of rock and hurled it with such force as to crush the skull of "the old grizzly." As Ten-ie-ya fell, other stones were cast upon him by the attacking party, after the Pai-ute custom, until he was literally stoned to death. All but eight of Ten-ie-ya's young braves were killed; these escaped down the valley, and through the cañon below.

The old men and women, who survived the first assault, were permitted to escape from the valley. The young women and children were made captives and taken across the mountains to be held as slaves or drudges to their captors.

EPILOG: THE TOURISTS' DISCOVERY

RECORDS of the number of visitors to the Yosemite down to and inclusive of 1875, show that in 1852 Rose and Shurban were murdered by the savages, while their companion, Tudor, though wounded, escaped. The next year, 1853, eight men from the North Fork of the Merced visited the valley, returning unharmed. Owing to murders of Starkey, Sevil and Smith, in the winter of 1853-4, as it was believed, by the Yosemites, no visitors entered the valley during the summer of 1854. In 1855 Messrs. Hutchings, Ayers, Stair and Milliard visited it without being disturbed by the sight of any of the original proprietors, either Indians or grizzlies. Mr. Hutchings, on his return to San Francisco, began to draw the attention of the public to the Yosemite, through his magazine and otherwise. Notwithstanding the ample means afforded by his magazine, and his facilities as a writer, Mr. Hutchings found it difficult to bring the valley into prominent and profitable notice, and few Californians could be induced to make it a visit. A peculiarity of those days was a doubt of the marvelous, and a fear of being "*sold.*" Any statements of travelers or of the press, that appeared exaggerated, were received by the public with extreme caution. Not more than twenty-five or thirty entered during that year, though Mr. Hutchings' efforts were seconded by reports of other visitors.

"FALL OF YA-NO-PAU", VERNAL FALL BY THOMAS AYRES, 1856

The following season, 1856, it was visited by ladies from Mariposa and San Francisco, who safely enjoyed the pleasures and *inconveniences* of the trip; aroused and excited to the venture, no doubt, by their traditional curiosity. The fact being published that ladies could safely enter the valley lessened the dread of Indians and grizzlies, and after a few *brave reports* had been published, this fear seemed to die away completely.

From this time on to 1864, a few entered every season; but during these times California had a *wonder* and interest in its population and their enterprises, greater than in any of its remarkable scenery. Everything was at high pressure, and the affairs of business and the war for the Union were all that could excite the common interest. In 1864, there were only 147 visitors, including men, women and children. The action of Congress this year, in setting the Yosemite and big trees apart from the public domain as national parks,* attracted attention to them. The publicity given to the valley by this act was world-wide, and since 1864 the number visiting it has steadily increased.

According to the *Mariposa Gazette,* an authentic record shows that in the season of 1865 the number was 276, in 1866, 382, in 1867, 435, in 1868, 627, and increasing rapidly; in 1875 the number for that year had reached about 3,000. The figures are deemed reliable, as they were obtained from the records of toll-roads and hotels. They are believed to be very nearly correct.

The *Gazette* "estimates the proportion of eastern and

---

*Today Yellowstone (established in 1872) is often credited as the first national park, on the basis that Congress' "Yosemite Grant" was State-administered. Bunnell and many other early writers, however, did not make this distinction and called Yosemite a national park.

European in the total number to be at least nine-tenths," and says: "It is safe to place the Atlantic and European visitors for the next ten years at 2,000 per annum."

But I must no longer dwell upon my theme, nor tell of the fruitful Fresno lands, redeemed from savage barbarity. Those scenes of beauteous enchantment I leave to those who may remain to enjoy them. And yet—

> El Capitan, I turn to gaze upon thy lofty brow,
> With reverent yearnings to thy Maker bow.
> But now farewell, Yosemite;
> If thou appearest not again in sight,
> Thou'lt come, I know, in life's extremity
> While passing into realms of light.

THE END.

"CASCADE OF THE RAINBOW", BRIDALVEIL FALL BY THOMAS AYRES, 1855